"Shaunti and Lisa have done an outstanding job talking about the issues, confusion, and dreams our kids face as they grow—and thus the issues we face as parents. Someone once said to me, 'God gives us the most important job in the world called parenting, and gives that job to inexperienced people.' That is so true. But as you understand the inner life of your child, you will be much better equipped to meet the challenges and joys of being a good parent. I encourage you to pick up this book and start the journey of understanding today."

—JIM DALY, president of Focus on the Family

"Shaunti and Lisa have boldly gone where no one has gone before: straight into the brain of a teenager! The insights they have found give us a unique peek into the hopes, fears, desires, and challenges facing the next generation. Savvy parents will read and respond to what they learn in this book, and their family will be better as a result."

—DENNIS RAINEY, president of FamilyLife

"I will be buying this book by the case. As a youth minister, I'm always trying to communicate to parents exactly what Shaunti and Lisa so eloquently and poignantly communicate in *For Parents Only*. Every parent of teens should read this brilliant book!"

—DANNAH GRESH, author of *And the Bride Wore White*

"Sandra and I love this book! With two teenage boys and a daughter who just started middle school, we soaked up Shaunti and Lisa's insights and discoveries like sponges. This is not just another book on parenting. It is a fascinating look at the way your child's mind works. We plan to use *For Parents Only* as a curriculum in our home group."

—ANDY STANLEY, pastor of North Point Community Church

"Shaunti and Lisa dive into the deepest core of kids' hearts to bring parents amazingly insightful truths and advice. They hit the bull's-eye when it comes to advice on raising children in the twenty-first century!"

—DR. JOE WHITE, president of Kanakuk Kamps

"At times I felt like I was sitting at a school lunch table, listening in on how kids really feel about their parents and what they would like to tell them. Shaunti and Lisa do an exceptional job of researching the topic and then making very practical suggestions. This gets my five-star rating on the HomeWord.com website."

—JIM BURNS, PH.D., president of HomeWord and author
of *Confident Parenting*

"I am so grateful for the hours of compassionate listening, ton of credible research, and weight of brutal honesty represented within the pages of this book. As a mother of three teenagers, I am the first to admit that I need help! Thank you, Shaunti and Lisa, for coming alongside on this wild, woolly, and wonderful adventure."

—LISA WHELCHEL, best-selling author of *Creative Correction,
The Busy Mom's Guide to Prayer,* and *Taking Care of the
"Me" in Mommy*

"*For Parents Only* beautifully breaks down the communication code between parents and children. Shaunti and Lisa consistently support their findings with extensive research and rock-solid solutions. This book delivers, and we highly recommend it!"

—DR. GARY and BARB ROSBERG, America's Family Coaches,
authors of *The 5 Sex Needs of Men and Women,* and cohosts
of *Dr. Gary and Barb Rosberg—Your Marriage Coaches*

"Shaunti Feldhahn's latest series of books have helped her readers unlock some of the mysteries of family relationships. Now she and Lisa Rice have given us keys to understanding our teenagers by hearing directly from them about *why* they do *what* they do. We only wish that this book had been written when our kids were younger!"

—BOB and CHERYL RECCORD, speakers and coauthors
of *Launching Your Kids for Life*

for parents only

getting inside the head of your kid

shaunti feldhahn
lisa a. rice

MULTNOMAH
BOOKS

FOR PARENTS ONLY
PUBLISHED BY MULTNOMAH BOOKS
12265 Oracle Boulevard, Suite 200
Colorado Springs, Colorado 80921
A division of Random House Inc.

Scripture quotations are taken from The Holy Bible, English Standard Version, copyright © 2001 by Crossway Bibles, a division of Good News Publishers. Used by permission. All rights reserved.

ISBN 978-1-59052-932-4

Library of Congress Cataloging-in-Publication Data
Feldhahn, Shaunti Christine.
   For parents only / Shaunti Feldhahn and Lisa A. Rice. — 1st ed.
       p. cm.
   Includes bibliographical references.
   ISBN 978-1-59052-932-4
 1. Parenting—Religious aspects—Christianity. 2. Child rearing—Religious aspects—Christianity. I. Rice, Lisa Ann. II. Title.
   BV4529.F45 2007
   248.8'45—dc22

                                             2007020265

Printed in the United States of America
2007—First Edition

10 9 8 7 6 5 4 3 2 1

To our parents,
Dick and Judy Reidinger and Glen and Lee Hultquist

It is said that the number one status symbol in America today
is no longer a big house or car, but longevity in marriage. This book
is dedicated to two great couples whose combined ninety-five years
of marriage have created an invaluable foundation for this book.

Contents

1   Looking In on Growing Up 1
    Taking a tour inside your kid's head and heart

2   Rebel with a Cause 13
    Why even good kids go crazy for freedom,
    and how to restore sanity

3   Who *Are* You? 39
    Why your child suddenly treats you like an alien—
    and acts like one too

4   The Good Thing About Being the Bad Guy 65
    Why your child secretly hopes you'll stand your ground

5   I Will Be Here for You 89
    How to help teens feel secure in the ascent to
    adulthood, even when they lose their footing

6   Can You Hear Me Now? 113
    Why your teen is convinced he can't talk to you,
    and how to change his mind

7   Attitude Adjustment 133
        *What mood swings reveal about teens' secret fears,
        and how you can boost their confidence*

8   In Case You Ever Wonder... 167
        What your child most wants to tell you

Afterword 175
Notes 177
Acknowledgments 180

One

LOOKING IN ON GROWING UP

Taking a tour inside your kid's head and heart

One recent fall weekend, I (Shaunti) went tent camping with my family and some good friends. With four couples and eight children under the age of seven, there was lots of laughter, not much sleep, and plenty of great memories.

One memory in particular will be burned into my brain for the rest of my life. After joining some other campers—a youth group—on a hayride, we all piled out of the wagon and began strolling back toward the camping area. One of the youth-group parents smiled at our small children. "Oh, enjoy this time, while they look like this," she said. Then she turned and gestured at the group of tall, lanky teenagers now walking far ahead of us on the rolling country road. "Because in the blink of an eye, they're going to look like that."

As if on cue, our little ones began to break free from our hands and skip ahead, first walking, then running down the hill. The rays of the setting sun seemed to capture a portrait of the small admirers racing toward the supercool teenagers…racing toward growing up. I couldn't stop the tears from leaping to my eyes.

Wherever You Are on the Road…

As I write this book with my friend Lisa, whose kids are long and lanky and off doing their own thing most of the time, we're both struck by the fleeting nature of childhood and sobered by our role in turning these dependent little people into healthy, independent adults.

Whether you're the parent of a small child or you only have a few months left until Junior leaves the nest, the goal of this book is to help you understand several key things that are likely going on— or soon will be—in the inner life of your child, some inner wiring that you may have never understood before.

As any parent can attest, there's a lot that we don't "get" about our children, a lot that leaves us feeling baffled. Why does a little girl who wants to be your best friend one minute become painfully embarrassed by your existence the next? What causes a normally good-natured teenager to yell something hot headed and even cruel, then run to his room and slam the door? What provokes a firmly grounded, responsible youth to start questioning everything your family believes in?

Most important, what do we do about it?

In the chapters ahead we're not going to focus as much on these confusing—even infuriating!—outward behaviors and attitudes as we are on the inner feelings, needs, and temptations that often *lead* to those behaviors. And as we do, we'll get a much clearer sense of what our kids need from us.

 The goal of this book is to help you understand several key things that are likely going on in the inner life of your child.

As parents, we are often so busy putting out fires that it's hard to be settled and confident in guiding children along the ups and downs of the road to adulthood. But our research has convinced us that once our eyes are opened to how our children are wired, we'll be better equipped not only to maximize but also to actually *enjoy* the precious time that we have with our children.

An ancient Hebrew proverb says, "Happy the generation where the great listen to the small, for it follows that in such a generation the small will listen to the great." That encapsulates the reason we've written this book. As we hear the dreams, concerns, and confusion common to so many of our kids, we'll learn how best to be an influence in their lives for years to come.

The People Behind the Book

Before we go too far, we should give you a bit of background. Shaunti is a public speaker, newspaper columnist, and the author of many best-selling books, including *For Women Only: What You Need to Know About the Inner Lives of Men* and its companion book, *For Men Only.* Lisa is a screenwriter, a youth speaker and leader, and the coauthor (with Shaunti) of *For Young Women Only: What You Need to Know About How Guys Think.* This series has been dedicated entirely to investigating and analyzing the key surprises about the people most important to us. And as sometimes-bewildered parents ourselves, we knew very early on that we needed to dig into those things that we just tend not to "get" about our kids.

As with the previous books, the eye-opening findings in these pages are entirely research based. We are not psychologists or family therapists. Rather, we are trained analysts just crazy enough to try to apply our skills and experience (Shaunti as a Harvard-trained analyst on Wall Street, Lisa as an appraiser conducting high-level business valuations) to helping people understand one another. And we think the best way we can serve parents who want to understand what's going on with their kids is by taking you directly to the *real* experts: the kids themselves.

At first, some observers questioned whether children could really speak about their inner lives with any sort of clarity. But in our research, we were amazed by the profound insights and often brilliant analysis the kids (primarily teens and preteens) offered into what's going on inside their hearts and minds—and what they most need from their parents.

 We were amazed by the profound insights and often brilliant analysis the kids offered into what's going on inside their hearts and minds.

At this point, you might already want to ditch a book that forces you to listen to teenagers, especially if you're having a bad week or thinking ungenerous thoughts about your blessed offspring. (Or are we the only ones who do that?) And we won't deny that some of what we heard from the kids was challenging. But overall, we think you'll be not only surprised by what these kids have to say, but also encouraged and better able to relate to your own kids…at least most of the time!

The Six Findings

So what are these surprising findings about the inner lives of our children? The chart below shows six areas in which parents often misunderstand what's happening with their kids when they hit the 'tween and teen years, and the surprising truths our research uncovered.

When They Hit the Teen Years	
Here's What We Think Is Happening	*Here's What's Really Happening*
Peer pressure pushes kids to rebel and behave in reckless ways without thinking through the consequences.	The intoxicating nature of freedom—and the fear of losing it—can lead even good kids to make choices that look like recklessness and rebellion, but directly addressing their craving for independence will help them build responsibility.
Teens seem to reject parents and their values, no longer caring much what their parents think.	Separating themselves from their parents' identity is one of the only ways healthy teenagers can develop their own; but even as they seem to push us away, our children still secretly want to know our values and need our affirmation of who they are becoming.
Teens don't want rules or discipline.	Although our teens test our authority and argue with rules, they secretly want us to stand firm as parents and will lose respect for us if we don't.

When kids make mistakes, they disregard their parents' opinions or criticism.	Although they may not look like it, kids want the security of knowing we are making the effort to understand them and will be there for them regardless of their mistakes—but kids will emotionally shut out a parent they see as judgmental.
Kids say parents don't listen.	Kids tend to stop talking because they perceive parents as rotten listeners but will open up when we prove we're safe and calmly acknowledge their feelings before addressing a problem.
Teens give in easily to negative attitudes—afflicting their families with sullenness, anger, or back talk—over what seem to be minor issues.	What looks like an attitude problem may actually be a sign of insecurity, but actively countering our children's fears can build their confidence and help them become more respectful of parents and others.

A Behind-the-Scenes Look

You might be wondering how we managed to wring all this information out of a bunch of monosyllabic adolescents. Well, first we conducted confidential focus groups with teens and preteens around the country. We also held numerous kid-on-the-street interviews, stopping teenagers in shopping malls, coffee shops, schools, and arcades to ask what they were really thinking and feeling about all sorts of issues. We dug into our files of input from hundreds of teenage guys for our earlier book *For Young Women Only* and followed up in more depth. Whenever either of us traveled for speaking events—from Los Angeles to Kansas City to Saratoga—we talked to kids to confirm that what we were hearing was fairly universal.

Finally, we conducted a groundbreaking, professional, nationally representative survey with the help of two sets of experts: Chuck Cowan at Analytic Focus—the former chief of survey design at the U.S. Census Bureau—and Kevin Sharp and Kelly Puig of the internationally renowned survey company Decision Analyst. In all, four hundred and twenty-seven anonymous kids across the country—ages fifteen, sixteen, and seventeen—answered roughly two dozen questions about how they think, what they feel, and what they need.*

The survey confirmed the results of our personal and group interviews. Not only did we hear the same things over and over from our young sages—reflected in the quotes you'll find in the following pages—but the personal stories and perspectives they shared with us were backed up by statistically valid evidence. In the end, this book incorporates the input and insight of more than twelve hundred kids.

We also asked some adult experts to help us make sense of what

---

* The scientific survey anonymously surveyed kids of all major racial groups, belief systems, and socioeconomic strata, and provided a 96 percent confidence level with a +/-3.5 percentage point variation.

we were hearing from the kids, and these consultants allowed us to pepper them with questions via e-mail, phone calls, and in-person discussions. These are not parenting experts so much as they are experts in understanding what's going on inside kids. We are indebted to, among others, Dr. Julie Carbery, PhD psychiatrist and child and family therapist who counsels troubled families; Nerida Edwards, nationally certified middle-school guidance counselor; Emerson Eggerichs, former pastor who now runs a national ministry to help the sexes understand each other and author of the best-selling book *Love and Respect;* and Vicki Courtney, founder of the Virtuous Reality organization for teen girls.

Before We Start

Before we take you inside your kid's head, we need to emphasize a few points:

1. *We are not endorsing the behavior or excusing the poor choices described by some kids in these pages.* Our goal is to serve as your tour guides through the strange and wonderful world of "teendom" and to give you new information to help you understand what's going on inside the kids, why they might do some insane things, and how these facts can give clearer direction to your parenting. We need to emphasize that just because certain thoughts and behaviors are seen over and over, we are *not* saying they are desirable or acceptable.

2. *Our findings are nationally representative, but we personally approach parenting from a Christian worldview.* We aim to lead our children toward choices that will help them reach their full, God-given potential. We want to help you do the same, and we believe our nationally representative findings and analysis will be helpful even if you do not share our worldview.

3. *This book is not just for parents of teenagers.* Although we were limited to surveying teens for legal reasons, and we focused the book on the most intense application of these truths in the 'tween and teen years, we believe parents of small children will find this advance information immensely valuable. As the mother of two young children, currently ages four and seven, I (Shaunti) can already see the application of several of these findings, and the value of laying the right foundation before the teen years arrive.

4. *There are exceptions to every rule.* When we say that most kids appear to think a certain way, realize that *most* means exactly that—most, not all. We're making generalizations out of necessity, and as the professional survey shows, there will be exceptions. (In addition, since some exceptions may include serious problems that are beyond the scope of this book, we strongly urge parents in those situations to seek guidance from a professional child and family therapist.)

5. *This book is not intended as a comprehensive overview of parenting principles.* Our sole goal is to open your eyes to several critical things that are likely to be going on inside your child, things that many parents tend not to "get." But new insights alone are rarely enough to change a life. Once you recognize certain realities, you may want to investigate the wonderful resources out there that address particular topics in more depth—especially those that explore God's power to transform the heart. (You'll find links to several resources—including our survey data—at www.forparents onlybook.com.) In addition, because our "what to do about it" sections can't cover the highly individual situations parents will encounter, we strongly suggest that you read with pencil in hand and make running notes about how you might apply a particular insight in your family. The companion *For Parents Only Discussion Guide* can help you put your new insights to work.

One last point: as you read, give yourself a break. None of us as parents can possibly measure up to everything we think we should do—or, for that matter, to all the things kids say they need. At the end of the movie *Cheaper by the Dozen,* the oldest daughter says to her dad (played by Steve Martin), "You taught me that there's no way to be a perfect parent, but there's a million ways to be a good one." We believe that if you're reading this book, you're already a good parent. Please keep the big picture in mind and avoid the temptation to judge your parenting or that of others. Because there's only one perfect parent...and we're not Him.

Both of us believe that although we may encounter some challenges along the way, there is also a heavenly Father guiding those who seek the truth. That may or may not be your worldview, but we hope our findings and analysis will be helpful no matter where you are in your own parenting journey.

So are you ready? Let's embark on a thrilling and sometimes scary adventure...inside the head of your kid.

Two

REBEL WITH A CAUSE

Why even good kids go crazy for freedom, and how to restore sanity

> The intoxicating nature of freedom—and the fear of losing it—can lead even good kids to choices that look like recklessness and rebellion, but directly addressing their craving for independence will help them build responsibility.

Do you know that our teens are addicted? They really are. The fact is, even if our kids have never touched an addictive substance, they're still hooked on something with a high far greater than anything a basement lab can conjure up.

This intoxicating agent is called freedom. And as it turns out, a lot of behavior that confuses and alarms parents can be tied directly to a child's desperate quest for the rush of freedom—and to his fear of losing it.

Before we understood this, we were puzzled by exchanges like the following, in which a sixteen-year-old boy passionately complained about how he was being disciplined:

> *Him:* "I hate when my parents take away my stuff,
> especially my cell phone or my computer. It's so unfair!"
> *Us:* "Do you think you didn't deserve that punishment?"
> *Him:* "I don't know. Maybe. But they just can't do
> that. That's *my* cell phone, man! That's *my* computer!
> They can't just take it away!"

After hearing this a few dozen times, we realized these comments signaled something beyond a teenager's obliviousness to the fact that Mom and Dad paid for the cell phone.

Freedom Is Like Cocaine

Enter Dr. Julie Carbery, adolescent and child psychotherapist, who has seen and heard it all in her twelve years of practice. We turned to her for help in identifying patterns in the teenage passions we were hearing. When we asked what was going on with this outraged sixteen-year-old and his fellow sufferers, she didn't hesitate.

"What's going on is freedom. Freedom is *cocaine* to a teenager. It's intoxicating. It's addictive. And it is often their biggest motivator. They will do anything to get it, and they are terrified of losing it. This cell phone kid is really saying, 'Don't you take away my cocaine! Don't you take away my freedom!'"

 "Freedom is *cocaine* to a teenager. It's intoxicating. It's addictive. And it is often their biggest motivator."

Eyes: open!

Once our eyes were opened, we watched in amazement at how often the addictive quest for freedom explained the motives and behaviors of the kids we talked to. "Addictive" may sound like an exaggeration, but look at how one representative high-school sophomore explained the feeling of freedom: "Once you have it, you can't get enough. Once you taste it, you want more and more." He concluded, "I can't *imagine* being supercontrolled anymore."

Almost all the kids we talked with described a desperate pursuit of the ability to control their own possessions, choose their own friends, stay up late, sleep over at any friend's house whenever they want, eat or drink what they want, drive where they want at the speed they want, and generally make their own choices apart from even the most well-intentioned parents.

This craving was demonstrated in our national survey, in which nearly three out of four kids said they were strongly motivated to pursue freedom, and only a tiny fraction didn't really care about having freedom at all.

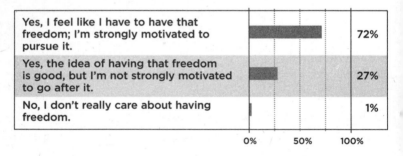

Is freedom something that motivates you and that you eagerly want? (For example, the ability to have your own cell phone, drive yourself places to do what you want to do, and so on.) Choose one answer.

Yes, I feel like I have to have that freedom; I'm strongly motivated to pursue it.	72%
Yes, the idea of having that freedom is good, but I'm not strongly motivated to go after it.	27%
No, I don't really care about having freedom.	1%

In other words, freedom is not just a big deal to kids; it's what gets them up and going in the morning. (Or noon.)

"Freeedooommm!"

At the end of the last day of school last year, I (Lisa) watched in amusement as the doors to the high school flew open and the kids erupted with their arms raised, yelling the *Braveheart* battle cry, "Freeedooommm!"

Freedom is not just a big deal to kids; it's what gets them up and going in the morning.

It appears that war-painted William Wallace's epic passion for freedom lives on in our very own rosy-cheeked offspring. As our teens experience their first exhilarating rush of freedom, they realize it feels insanely good. Once they taste it, they want more. And more.

"It gives me such a sense of power."

People who use drugs or alcohol are seeking a temporary, exhilarating high—often described as the feeling of being able to do things they normally couldn't. Our kids are getting the same rush, but in a good way. They're experiencing the thrill of freedom, of being liberated to do things on their own, often for the first time!

Keep in mind that for their whole lives our children have been dependent on us in countless ways. If your daughter wanted to go to the movies, she had no way to get there without you. If your son desperately wanted to play on the soccer team, he had to rely on you for the necessary money and transportation. Even if your daughter simply wanted to talk with a friend about homework, she first had to be sure you didn't need the house phone at that moment. And if you suddenly did need to make a call, she had to wrap up her conversation.

Freedom

You can see why finally being able to do things on their own is such a thrill for our kids. Look how passionately several teenagers described their relief at no longer being dependent:

- "It took me three years to save up for my car, and now that I have it, I feel so released. Whenever it's stressful around the house, I just take off and drive, top down, wind blowing, music blaring, and everything's better. I feel sorry for my friends that don't have wheels. I'll do anything to make sure I've got my own car handy."

- "It gives me such a *sense of power* to be able to schedule my own time and do what I want" (emphasis ours).

- "There was such tension building up inside me before I got my license, like I was ready to explode from having to depend on someone else to get me places. I'm much more relaxed now."

"I felt like a real person."

Freedom not only gives your child the powerful relief of no longer being dependent, it also gives him the thrill of being an independent agent out there in the world as his own person, without having life filtered through you as the middleman. Consider this revealing comment: "When I finally got my own cell phone, everything changed. I felt like a real person, suddenly connected directly to my friends and the world through phone calls and text messages. I can't imagine living without that."

Once a kid enjoys the entrancing feeling of being a "real person," you can see how scary it would be to think of losing that feeling.

"I should be able to make my own decisions."

Kids who begin to feel they don't need a physical middleman anymore (a.k.a. Mom or Dad) quickly begin to resist and resent being controlled by that middleman as well. Look at the telling way one teen describes this frustration:

> It makes me mad when my parents try to control who I talk to at night on the cell phone. I mean, if I'm keeping my grades up, why should they care if I stay up late talking and lose a little sleep? I have to keep up with my friends, or I go nuts. The decision should be up to *me*.

The Five Facts of Freedom

When we see our teens pushing the independence envelope, taking foolish risks, evading straight answers, or breaking rules, we often chalk it up to peer pressure, media influence, and even rebellion—and we come down hard. Sometimes, obviously, there is a rebellious heart that needs to be dealt with, and lowering the boom may be necessary. But if we can spot the much more common signs of a spirit that is simply straining for a healthy freedom (albeit imperfectly), we can guide our child's quest in ways that are healthy instead of

Freedom

counterproductive—helping them learn responsibility instead of triggering their sense of desperation.

We found five often-overlooked truths about this freedom-seeking aspect of a child's inner life.

Fact #1: Freedom wields a greater influence than parents or peers.

Over the years, many studies (and parents!) have asked whether parents or peers exert a bigger influence on kids' behavior. Our research convinced us that this question misses the main point. When freedom is added to the mix, it seems to far outstrip the influence of any person. Look at the astounding survey results.

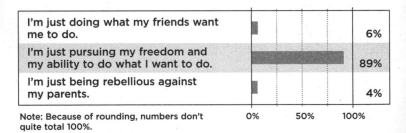

When you do something that your parents would disapprove of, what is the best description for the reason that you do it? Choose one answer.

I'm just doing what my friends want me to do.	6%
I'm just pursuing my freedom and my ability to do what I want to do.	89%
I'm just being rebellious against my parents.	4%

Note: Because of rounding, numbers don't quite total 100%.

0%   50%   100%

Nine out of ten kids said that when they do something questionable, it's not primarily because of peer pressure or because they are rebelling against parents; it's because they are pursuing their freedom and their ability to do what *they* want to do. And although parents with strong faith beliefs might wish otherwise, this dynamic wasn't markedly different among kids who described themselves as Christians attending church every week.

It's all about doing what they want.

We heard from the kids that although both peer pressure and parental expectation have influence, neither is usually the motivator that freedom is. Peer or parental pressure is imposed from the outside, while the desire for freedom comes from the inside. When the two are in conflict, the internal "want" often wins.

For example, one girl described a typical peer-pressure situation: a school dance, where she didn't want to "dirty dance" with a guy, but her close friend did. The first girl repeatedly told her friend it wasn't cool and asked her not to dance that way—but it didn't matter. The friend did as she wanted—and accepted that the first girl would be upset with her for a while. At that moment, the opinion of her peer was a lesser factor than doing what *she* wanted to do; in other words, a lesser factor than freedom.

They also realize they can.

Allied to the powerful pressure of *wanting* to do something is the potent realization that they *can*. We talked to so many "good" kids who confessed to doing at least some things that their parents wouldn't approve of. They described the intoxicating realization that, physically, they could do what they want to do—because no one could really stop them.

On our survey, nearly seven out of ten kids admitted they would find a way to do something they wanted to do, even if their parents might disapprove.

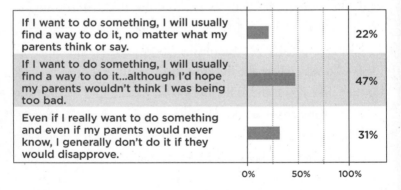

Think of something that you really want to do that your parents might disapprove of. Which statement most closely describes you? Choose one answer.

If I want to do something, I will usually find a way to do it, no matter what my parents think or say.	22%
If I want to do something, I will usually find a way to do it...although I'd hope my parents wouldn't think I was being too bad.	47%
Even if I really want to do something and even if my parents would never know, I generally don't do it if they would disapprove.	31%

Here's what one representative teenage guy told us: "I'll stop at nothing to get my way. I might make a slight modification based on my parents' wishes, but yeah, I'll do what I want."

This is the stark truth: Short of locking our teenagers in their rooms day and night, there is almost no way to physically prevent them from doing what they want to do. And they know it.

Now, most of the kids in our survey consoled themselves with the hope (perhaps wishful thinking!) that their parents wouldn't think they were being too bad. In other words, although most kids still care what their parents think, less than a third will let it stop them from doing something they want to do.

 "I might make a slight modification based on my parents' wishes, but yeah, I'll do what I want."

We should, however, mention one heartening exception. In most cases, the focus groups and survey found very few differences between kids who had a strong faith influence and those who didn't. But this is one of the few cases in which a difference did jump out at us: kids in private Protestant Christian schools were almost the reverse of those in any other kind of school (public, Roman Catholic, other private academies). Among the small number of kids attending private, Protestant Christian schools (6 percent of our sample), nearly two-thirds would stop themselves from doing something they wanted to do if they felt their parents would disapprove.

Fact #2: Under the influence of freedom, kids may do stupid things.

Like addicts under the influence of a real drug, kids high on the thrill of freedom may not be thinking clearly. To complicate matters, it's not just the high of freedom at work.

Freedom

It turns out—and we say this as respectfully as possible—our teens are not only addicted; they are also brain deficient. Science demonstrates that the frontal lobe of the brain—the area that allows judgment of consequences and control of impulses—doesn't fully develop until after the teen years. So in the absence of a fully functioning frontal lobe, teenage brains rely more on the centers that control emotion—which in effect means they give in much more easily to impulses.

Teenagers also subconsciously believe they are invincible, that nothing bad will happen if they drive too fast in the rain, become sexually involved, or get drunk and go swimming in the lake with their friends.

So kids who are operating under the influence of freedom, feel they are invincible, *and* suffer from incomplete brain wiring will sometimes disregard rules and consequences to do really stupid things.

 The frontal lobe of the brain—the area that allows judgment of consequences and the control of impulses—doesn't fully develop until after the teen years.

We asked every focus group this question: "What if a hidden camera followed you and your friends for one week?" Without exception, every teenager gasped or groaned. When we pressed for details, almost every child provided examples of using bad language, lying, smoking, cheating, experimenting with sex, breaking curfew, or driving recklessly.

Trying not to gasp ourselves, we asked the kids, "Why do you do these things?"

The typical answer (again): "Because we want to, and we can." (And, brain scientists would add, because their brains are not yet wired to easily stop themselves!)

Now, before we move on, remember that we are not excusing poor choices. But this does help us understand *why* those poor choices sometimes get made.

Fact #3: Kids deeply fear losing their freedom.

Once we understand just how much teenagers revel in their first tastes of real freedom, it shouldn't be surprising that, like other addicts, they're also dealing with deep fear that we will forever take that freedom away. An enraged teenager's out-of-proportion response to your words or actions may be a sign that you've set off her ultrasensitive "loss of freedom" radar.

So what most pushes a kid's fear buttons?

- *The sense that freedom has been snatched arbitrarily.* Most kids said that they felt their freedom was often taken away for no good reason or with no consistent pattern, and they were thus overly sensitive to the mention of possible restrictions.

Freedom

- *Seeing their social life sabotaged.* Kids seem terrified that parental restrictions will make them outcasts— a fate worse than death for a fifteen-year-old. One kid declared, "When they ground you for so long, it's social suicide, and of course you sneak out. You've got to cover your rear and protect your life."

- *Not understanding the rules.* We'll cover this in a later chapter, but as Dr. Carbery notes, "When kids say, 'That punishment was so unfair,' it actually means, 'I wish I understood the reasons for those rules.' If they don't understand the reasons, what their highly emotional and irrational brains hear is, 'I'm going to control you for no reason.'"

Fact #4: Teens will do anything to get freedom and avoid losing it—including deceiving themselves and you.

Driven by the all-consuming quest for freedom and the intense fear that we'll revoke it, even teenagers who are generally good and trustworthy sometimes resort to bad behavior. They may downplay problems, fool themselves into thinking that they weren't doing anything wrong, hide things, and even lie to us—all in an effort to secure and protect their independence.

"What's the big deal?"

First, like other addicts, our kids may try to delude themselves—and us—into believing they don't really have a problem. For example, one afternoon, I (Lisa) got an uncharacteristic call from one of my daughters. She said, "Mom, I'm still planning to spend the night at Jessica's, but just FYI, I had the teeniest little boo-boo where I backed into this lady's headlight. I don't think it's a big deal, and you might not even need to come over here…"

In her eagerness to gloss things over, my daughter neglected to mention that this teeny boo-boo happened while she was breaking our rule of not talking on her cell phone while driving. She clearly wanted to assure me that this wasn't a big enough deal for me to bother with or—heaven forbid—impose penalties that would interfere with the planned sleepover! (More on my response later.)

One clever cousin to downplaying is to create nice, logical-sounding rationalizations. One family we know has a strict rule that the kids keep Mom and Dad informed about the "five *W*s" of their plans: who, what, when, where, and why. The dad was astonished to learn, therefore, that instead of being out at the approved movie the night before, his daughter had gone to a fairly wild party. Not to worry, she had an explanation: "The movie was sold out, so we went to Starbucks across the street. Then these guys we knew came by— the guys you met and liked from the Academy, remember?—well, my cell phone was dead, and I figured you and Mom were asleep anyway. And I knew you liked the guys…" This girl had fooled herself into thinking it was okay to break the family rules—and rationalized her way into a potentially dangerous situation.

Dr. Carbery (who, trust us, is no pushover!) assured us that many times such teens aren't being deliberately deceptive. Their train of thought truly leads in this direction, and they need help understanding why something shouldn't have been rationalized.

The hiding game.

Of course, sometimes the deception is intentional. In order to protect their freedoms, 83 percent of the kids we surveyed admitted hiding things from their parents.

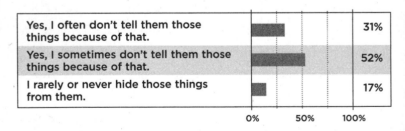

Do you ever hide negative information from your parents because you're worried about how they will react? Choose one answer.

Yes, I often don't tell them those things because of that.	31%
Yes, I sometimes don't tell them those things because of that.	52%
I rarely or never hide those things from them.	17%

We found very little difference between kids who attended church weekly and those who held no particular religious beliefs.

But there was, again, a distinct difference among the small subset of kids attending private Protestant Christian schools. It turns out that "only" half of those kids said they would hide things. Ah, well.

Obviously, one type of hiding is simply failing to mention an infraction, so the parent never hears about it. But this comment from a teen girl reflects the more "active" examples we heard from many of her peers: "If my mom won't let me wear a spaghetti-strap shirt, I'll just put it on under a loose, dumpy shirt and wave good-bye to my mom. Then, as soon as I get to school, the big shirt comes off."

Liar, liar!

The most insidious tactic, of course, is outright deception. And when we asked the teens why they lie, they basically all said the same thing as this boy: "Because parents will freak out about the truth."

We found that some forms of teenage lying are fiendishly clever. One boy we'll call Ken told us about being at his girlfriend's house, which was a violation of his parents' rules. When his mother called his cell phone to check up on him, he fibbed, "Hi, Mom. Yes, I'm at Jonathan's... You want to talk to him? Well, you can't right now. He's in the other room...with a girl. You understand..." The next day Ken's mom had the proverbial sex talk with Jonathan, much to the guys' amusement.

The kids also described common untruths that most parents will buy, such as, "We're at the movies, and there's an hour left.

Freedom

When it's over, I'll be right home." After all, what kind of unmerciful parent would yank their child out of a movie that's only halfway over?

Fact #5: Ironically, too much freedom can be scary, and our kids want to involve us in their quest.

After this fairly brutal reality check, the good news is that even freedom-intoxicated teens realize that unlimited freedom isn't a good idea.

One girl eloquently captured the perspective so many teens shared with us—and which we'll cover in more depth later: "My parents are really strict, and I wish they'd lighten up a bit. But if they didn't give me rules, I'd know they didn't love me. We expect some boundaries."

We were also thankful to hear that kids didn't always *want* to hide things or lie to their parents. In fact, they'd much prefer to talk to their parents about the choices and challenges they face, if they could do so "safely."

Kids didn't always *want* to hide things or lie to their parents. They'd prefer to talk to their parents if they could do so "safely."

What's a Parent to Do?

As I (Shaunti) read about the freedom-seeking teenagers that my sweet little kids will soon grow into, I felt a strong desire to climb into bed and pull the covers over my head! But since that's hardly a viable reaction, what *can* we do?

First off, it may help to realize that the desperate pursuit of independence is nothing new. In its selfish form, it's been causing problems since the human race first arrived on the planet. And as our kids seek a positive, necessary form of freedom, we can look for ways to help them understand the deeper spiritual need revealed by that craving and point them toward healthy ways to satisfy it.

Thankfully, the kids themselves offered a lot of wisdom for this process, starting with the appeal to neither give them all the freedom they want nor clamp down so hard that they're dying to get away. Instead, they say, we can help them learn to want the right things and to handle their independence responsibly. Let's look at how we can do exactly that.

1. Get to know your teen.

One of the most common appeals we heard from the teenagers was for parents to see them as individuals and understand how they're wired. Quite simply, some children can handle more freedom than others.

Freedom

As we noted in the introduction, we suggest going through the points of this chapter with an eye toward what lessons they hold for your response to *your* individual child. But next, consider asking yourself some pointed questions before giving a thumbs-up or thumbs-down to a request. Questions like: How responsible is this child? Is he cognitively able to process consequences yet, or does he still give in to impulses easily? Does he choose good friends? What do other adults think of him?

As we look for evidence of growing maturity, recent events can provide insight. Does she lose her cell phone weekly? If your son can't turn in his math homework, is he really responsible enough to be trusted with your car?

One particularly helpful exercise is to determine which of these two actual teen comments sounds most like your child:

- "I have to admit that if my parents were more lenient, I'd take advantage of it."
- "I'd never take advantage of them. I enjoy their trust and my wide leash."

2. Choose discipline with their key fear-triggers in mind.

The fear of losing freedom often explains why a teenager's reaction seems way out of proportion to a given situation. And knowing what freedoms are most important to your child will help you avoid unintentionally triggering her fight-or-flight instincts. For example, one child might view her cell phone as her lifeline to the world and as vital to her identity as a "real person." For another teen, the use of the car may be a far more critical tool of independence.

Since we usually have multiple discipline options at our disposal for a given infraction, it may be most productive to focus on the option that brings home the consequences without setting off the "loss of freedom" radar. Sometimes the loss of freedom is itself the appropriate consequence, but we want to exercise it wisely, understanding that for our child it is the "nuclear bomb" of discipline.

 Knowing what freedoms are most important to your child will help you avoid unintentionally triggering her fight-or-flight instincts.

For example, after my (Lisa's) daughter's car accident, I realized that the most effective consequence was not taking away her phone. Instead, we required her—and she preferred!—to pay the eight hundred dollars for repairs on the other driver's headlight. That meant four months of work with little take-home pay for herself, but she internalized an excellent lesson without the resentment that might have built up from a lengthy grounding or loss of cell phone privileges.

3. Set specific expectations.
Your kid will tend to feel more settled and secure—and be more honest with you—if he understands exactly what circumstances will

Freedom

result in his losing a particular freedom and what circumstances won't. For example, if your child feels particularly possessive about his cell phone, establish that it is for your convenience as his parent, and if he doesn't answer your calls or if he abuses his minutes, the phone will be taken away. But if he sticks to the rules, he can rest assured his cell phone privileges are secure.

Teen expert Vicki Courtney saw the power of establishing clear expectations when her kids started using the Internet. Setting the ground rules, she told them, "Now that you're going online, it's not a matter of *if* you'll be made uncomfortable, it's *when*. I know you can accidentally stumble onto bad sites, and I know that bad people can contact you. If a porn ad pops up, or if someone contacts you and makes you feel uncomfortable, let me know so I can figure out how it happened. I promise I will not take your Internet away."

Some time later, her daughter was contacted by someone who seemed threatening. When she approached Vicki to talk about it, the first thing she said was, "Uh, Mom, remember when you said you wouldn't take my Internet away?"

"If someone contacts you and makes you feel uncomfortable, let me know. I promise I will not take your Internet away."

As Vicki told us, "We have the freedom to discuss these things now because my kids know I'm not going to ban the Internet because of something they couldn't help, or because they made a mistake."

And since gaining freedom is a huge incentive, you might want to help your child realize that he'll have more freedom if he shows he can handle it—and that purposeful deception is the quickest way to lose it.

4. Equip them to cope wisely with their growing freedoms.

We've seen that seven out of ten kids will do what they want to do, no matter what we say. Even the fear of their parents' finding out doesn't compel them to stop their behavior, only to hide it. (Scary!) So we need to help our teens *want* to do the right things and not want the wrong ones. Beyond consistent, fervent prayer—which we advocate wholeheartedly—here are a few suggestions for pointing them in the right direction.

Help your kids learn to think through their decisions—and see where they might have been wrong.

As we'll detail in another chapter, the kids said they have to understand the reasons for the rules—embracing the rules for themselves and not thinking of them as being externally imposed. In addition, since the frontal lobe of your child's brain is probably underdeveloped, she may need you to act as an "external frontal lobe" to help

Freedom

her think through consequences. ("If you go to the mall, what does that mean for how much time you'll have to do your homework?") Similarly, your child could easily be deluding herself about whether a choice she already made was actually a bad one or whether it involved deception.

Although it may seem that she should already know what's right, give her some guidance anyway. Even mature teenagers may need an adult's help from time to time to look back on a given choice and recognize where their train of thought derailed. The kids suggested asking good questions ("Did you think of which kids might turn up at the party?") instead of giving a lecture, so that your child can work through the issue and draw a conclusion for herself.

Even mature teenagers may need an adult's help from time to time to look back on a given choice and recognize where their train of thought derailed.

This may also be why so many kids urged parents to let their kids learn on their own, even through their mistakes. One boy said his father often says to him, "It's your decision whether it's wise to go. I will allow it, but if you get in trouble, you will have to pay your own consequences."

Help them move from fearing parents to fearing God.

On the survey, we were surprised that fully six in ten kids said they consider whether God sees everything they do when they're tempted to do something that might be wrong. And among those God-aware kids, six in ten also said that the fact that God might be disappointed in them was a bigger influence than whether their parents would be disappointed. Parents can help such kids transition from fear of Mom and Dad to fear of God.

The fact that God might be disappointed in them was a bigger influence than whether their parents would be disappointed.

I (Lisa) saw this principle in action when I overheard my kids asking their dad if they could do something, and he answered, "You know your mom wouldn't like that!" Without looking up, I casually answered, "Oh, it's not about me. I'm not the ultimate One they have to answer to in the end. They'll have to talk to God about their choices." Later that night I was amazed when two of the girls separately came to me, saying that they felt God was urging them to be careful about certain friends and activities. His view of their actions had a far greater effect on them than I realized.

Freedom

———

As we watch our cherished no-longer-little ones begin the process of flying free, what a comfort it is to entrust them to the One who made them and to know that he holds them securely in his hands.

Although it may be scary to watch your child venture toward adulthood as an independent person, one thing the kids said was scary for them was figuring out who on earth that independent person *is*. That's the subject of our next chapter.

Three

WHO *ARE* YOU?

*Why your child suddenly treats you
like an alien—and acts like one too*

> Separating themselves from their parents'
> identity is one of the only ways healthy
> teenagers can develop their own; but
> even as they seem to push us away, our
> children still secretly want to know our
> values and need our affirmation of who
> they are becoming.

Not long ago, Lisa and I (Shaunti) returned from an out-of-town speaking engagement. As we walked through the door of my house, my kids were bouncing with delight. My son reached up his little three-year-old arms, pulled my face toward his, and gave me a big smack on the lips. My six-year-old daughter then plopped herself on my lap and hugged my neck as she giggled uncontrollably. I was in heaven.

In the midst of our precious encounter, I heard Lisa, in her most innocent voice, ask, "Can you believe that those sweet little lips will one day be lipping off to you?"

I glared at her, but she just let loose an evil, unapologetic, knowing laugh. This experienced mother of teens assured me that sweet-talking, sweet-kissing little ones do often grow into exasperating creatures who love us one minute and talk back the next. She confidently predicted that these children I know so intimately will one day exclaim, "You just don't understand me!" right before they stomp off to their rooms.

Now, perhaps like you, Jeff and I prefer to cling to the hope that our dear friend Lisa is just completely wrong—that this will never happen to *our* kids. But…what if she's *right*? I'm so glad our teenage focus groups offered fresh insight for perplexed parents who wonder what on earth happened to their once-adoring children.

As one of our friends says of her fifteen-year-old daughter, "I never know what's going to walk through the door after school. Half the time I think, *Who are you, and what have you done with my kid?!*"

"Half the time I think, *Who are you, and what have you done with my kid?!*"

As it turns out, that's exactly the question the kids themselves are asking.

"Who in the World Am I?"

What we saw over and over again in our research is that most teenagers are desperately flailing to be somebody—*their own somebody*—and that the sometimes painful ways they pull away from us are simply indicators of this internal journey.

We all know that children go through various developmental stages. In grade school and some of middle school, our kids want to be just like Mom and Dad, to identify with us as they learn what it means to be a woman or a man. But somewhere around age twelve (eleven for some kids, thirteen for others) it's almost like a switch gets flipped. Our children rapidly transition into a developmental stage in which the major, overriding, internal question of their lives transitions from *What is it like to be Mom or Dad?* to *Who in the world am I?*

Now they want to *stop* identifying with Mom and Dad and begin figuring out their own identity. Suddenly that little girl who wanted to dress just like you has become a bundle of adolescent nerves who wouldn't be caught dead in the matching outfits you bought just a few months ago. The little boy who begged to help Dad out in his workshop now requires a buffer zone of at least thirty feet so no one at the mall will think he's with you.

Identity

The major, overriding, internal question of their lives transitions from *What is it like to be Mom or Dad?* to *Who in the world am I?*

We often don't realize that when our children seem embarrassed by us, are hostile toward us, or—most worrisome—begin to question the values that they've been taught their whole lives, it is usually directly related to a search for themselves. They are not deliberately trying to hurt us. But because *our* identity—which they have been internalizing for the last thirteen years—is the only one they've ever known, they need to gain some distance from it in order to establish their own sense of self.

"I love you, but I'm not you."

The survey results demonstrated the universal nature of this drive:

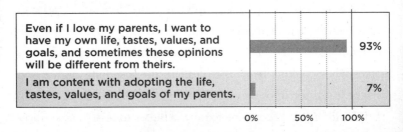

Which of the following best describes how you feel?
Choose one answer.

Even if I love my parents, I want to have my own life, tastes, values, and goals, and sometimes these opinions will be different from theirs.	93%
I am content with adopting the life, tastes, values, and goals of my parents.	7%

The vast majority of kids feel compelled to become their own person, with tastes, values, and goals that may be different from those of their parents—and by the time they hit seventeen years old, the number rises to nearly 100 percent. As one friend recently heard from her teen daughter, "I love you, Mom, but I'm not you. You got to be you, and I get to be me."

Now, before you go wrap yourself in your child's old blankie and cry yourself to sleep, let's remember why this reaction from our kids is not only necessary but actually healthy.

First word...first steps...first realization that we're mortifyingly uncool.

Since this is a developmental stage like any other, it's part of the road that kids must navigate on their way to healthy adulthood. Remember how amazing it was to watch your baby hit all those developmental milestones: his first step, his first word, his last diaper? (Woo-hoo!) As hard as it may be to believe, the first signs that your child is becoming his own person are just as worthy of celebration. The fledgling is stretching his wings and needs your guidance in learning to fly, rather than your determination to keep him earthbound.

By wisely guiding our children through this pulling-away stage, we'll help them take life steps that are just as critical as learning to lace up their own shoes. So let's look together at the surprising truths

Identity

we learned about how this stage impacts our children's thought processes and behaviors.

Finding Their Way by Questioning Yours

We strongly believe that understanding and making allowance for your children's identity-seeking process will eliminate a lot of angst. (That's code for: you'll know the reasons behind some confusing behaviors that would otherwise leave you tearing out your hair!) And working within these realities will help ensure that you remain an essential part of the process as your child grows into the person that she will be for the rest of her life.

Reality #1: For a time, your kids will question and sometimes even reject the only identity they have known, which is yours.

Okay, so we know in theory that kids need to find their own identity. What we often don't realize is that the processes they go through may feel an awful lot like rejection to us. Is there any parent of a teenager who hasn't repeatedly heard, "You just don't understand me!" Or even, "Please drop me off at the corner," with the unspoken reason being, *so my friends won't see you.*

Rest assured that while your hormone-saturated teenager could perhaps choose nicer ways to express herself, the feelings behind the words are both normal and an important part of her healthy search for personal identity.

 We know in theory that kids need to find their own identity. What we often don't realize is that the process they go through may feel an awful lot like rejection to us.

Dismantling your castle.

To illustrate why this questioning is so necessary, let's imagine a playroom scenario. Suppose you built a beautiful castle out of building blocks and brought over your preschooler to show off your finished masterpiece. Would your child stand back and say, "Wow, Mommy, that's the best thing I've ever seen—I couldn't possibly improve upon perfection"? Or would he gleefully knock it over, sit down, and then build his own?

In the same way, your teen or preteen child is building his own castle, but—and here's the key—he has no raw materials of his own. All he has are *your* building blocks: values, ideals, opinions, and ways of behaving that you (and others close to him) have built into his mind and heart to this point in his life. Sure, he's had the power of independent choice from the earliest age, but he didn't begin to crave an independent identity until that critical eleven- to thirteen-year-old benchmark.

Identity

The only way your child can build his own castle is to dismantle what you and other influencers have built and to restructure those materials into something all his own. And as he does so, he'll hold each building block at arm's length and examine it from various angles while thinking—perhaps subconsciously—*I've heard this all my life. I know this is part of who my parents and teachers are, but is it part of who I am?*

The only way your child can build his own castle is to dismantle what you and other influencers have built and to restructure those materials into something all his own.

"This is how our family builds castles!"

Taking the analogy further, what if you were to rush over and stop your child from pulling down your castle? What if you said, "No, no, Johnny! Don't change a thing. This is how our family builds castles!"

Preschooler Johnny would frown or maybe throw a tantrum. Teenage Johnny may not say a word. But now he'll feel even *more* compelled to dismantle whichever building blocks you most want to keep intact. You've just made clear that those blocks, those parts of his internal castle, belong to you, not him. So he has an even more urgent need to pull them out (privately, next time), hold them up for inspection, and figure out if they are his blocks too...or if they are solely yours.

He'll feel even *more* compelled to dismantle whichever building blocks you most want to keep intact.

Often, a kid who is pushed hard toward a particular identity will completely reject it just to become his own person. One teenage girl touched on this instinctive resistance to being told who to be: "I hate those stage mothers who are living their lives through their kids. They don't get it that kids hate that. We have to be our own people. That kid is gonna run the other direction as soon as she can."

The not-so-sweet sounds of demolition.

Some verbal signals—"Dad, I want to be my own person!"—are obvious cues that a child has begun the dismantling process. Others are more subtle and potentially more hurtful, but they make a lot more sense when run through the "identity translation filter." For example:

"You're so embarrassing!" Have you ever wondered why your teenager finds you so profoundly embarrassing? It turns out that viewing you as embarrassingly outdated is one of the quickest ways for your child to see herself as different from you and to achieve the needed sense of separation. She's saying, "I'm trying to be cool. You represent the only identity I've ever known, so in order to rapidly distance myself from that old identity, I have to view you as so *un*cool that you're actually embarrassing."

Identity

During our focus groups, the kids tried to outdo each other with amusing examples of their parents' uncoolness. Said one girl, "My mom sings aloud to the Muzak songs in the grocery store. She thinks that the other customers are smiling *with* her, but they are clearly laughing *at* her."

"Oh, Mom, look at those pants!" Another signal of identity building is when those oh-so-sweet teenagers enjoy directly poking fun at their parents. For example, one day I (Lisa) was dancing around in some old jeans, and my daughters started laughing. Hannah said, "Um, Mom…how old are those pants?"

"I don't know." I glanced down. "Not more than fifteen years, I think."

"Well, um…do you have a minute to come and see a video?"

She and Sarah pulled up an online video called "Mom Jeans," which pokes fun at the typical attire of middle-aged females, including pants with high waists, nine-inch zippers, unflared legs, and the liberal inclusion of elastic. As the video played, my girls howled with laughter and pointed at me!

Afterward they said, "Mom, we'll take you shopping if you promise to throw away your Mom pants." True to their word, they got me some cool jeans from American Eagle. I was the only mother in the dressing room, but I must admit, I do like my new look.

Now they find other things to make fun of me about.

"I'm not even sure I believe what you believe." This is one of the hardest things for a parent to hear. Everything is relative in the later teen years; this "whatever" stage kicks in about ages sixteen to twenty. According to the experts, this is an actual developmental stage characterized by rampant relativism, where even a child with strong convictions might start saying things like, "Well, that's true for you, but I'm not sure it's true for me."

 Even a child with strong convictions might start saying things like, "Well, that's true for you, but I'm not sure it's true for me."

The good news, as we'll show you shortly, is that this relativism is tempered by a deep desire for the strongly held values and sense of heritage that most families try to provide.

Reality #2: Kids decide which identity points to keep based on their respect for primary influencers.

You could easily assume that your child is questioning only the parts of his identity connected with you while accepting everything else. You might also think that because he's questioning your precepts he's rejecting all of them. Neither is true.

Instead, the identity-building years are a time when teens watch and assess all the influences around them, including parents, other adults, and their many peers.

Looking for a reaction.

Part of this assessment involves "social referencing": determining how to react by watching the reactions of others. When a toddler falls down and looks to see whether Mom gasps in alarm before he decides to cry, that's social referencing.

The movie *Never Been Kissed* shows a typical teenage version. When the character played by Drew Barrymore suggests a prom theme, the whole class watches to see how the most popular guy in school responds before committing themselves. Only after he smiles and says, "Absolutely!" does everyone else quickly nod their okay.

Inside your teenager, two types of social referencing are helping him figure out who he wants to be:

- In *positive social referencing,* kids move toward those they admire, copying their behaviors and attitudes. At age thirteen, I (Shaunti) distinctly remember realizing that the other kids treated me better when I acted in ways similar to particular, well-liked classmates. So guess what I did?

- Via *negative social referencing,* however, kids move away from behaviors or labels they dislike. For example, we were sad to hear one girl say, "I'm not the goody-goody they think I am." In other words, "My parents' and teachers' identity for me is as an ultragood girl, but I'm not going to be that. As a matter of fact, let me prove how bad I can be."

Both referencing types have pros and cons. Positive referencing can provide a bad result if the child admires the neighborhood's macho gang leaders. And negative referencing can be valuable if he notices that whiners never have any friends and resolves to be cheerful himself.

How things shake out often depends on how teens feel about the influencers in their lives. Although a teen is watching her parents closely, she's unlikely to say straight out, "Dad, what do you think about…?" Instead, she might tell a story. "You know what happened at work? This guy fudged his hours on his timecard…"

She'll then note Dad's reaction—"That sounds like stealing to me; what do you think?"—and add that to her stack of potential building blocks. If she has a generally high opinion of Dad, she's more likely (although not certain) to adopt his perspective.

The peer mirror.

In addition to observing peers and parents for clues to acceptable behavior, teens are watching how others—especially peers—react to them.

In a way, peer relationships provide a mirror that shows them who they are. What they observe in their peers' reactions to the way they dress or interact online helps determine how they see themselves. To a certain degree, kids will see themselves as stylish or outdated, athletic or awkward, depending on how others view them.

They also look at themselves and ask, *Is what I have good enough to attract attention from the opposite sex?* And of course, peer reactions are the main mirror for that question.

Identity

Look at our revealing exchange with one teenage girl:

> *Her:* "Yeah, I'm a butter face."
> *Us,* confused: "What's a butter face?"
> *Her:* "It's what guys say: everything about her looks good 'but her face.' That's me."

The outward trappings of their inner decisions.

As our kids examine the question "Who am I?" they feel a strong need to present their ongoing answers to the world. Anything with the power to express "This is who I am"—such as their e-mail address, blog, web page, room, clothes, even their activities or skills—is absolutely critical to their sense of self.

We should also note that the kids seemed to harbor a deep fear of losing their embryonic sense of self, which is probably why they are so intensely protective of these outward trappings. As one kid told us, "My parents keep wanting me to take things off my MySpace, but they don't understand that that's an extension of *me*. If we aren't allowed on the outside to be who we are on the inside, we'll just end up getting lost in the crowd."

The Ties That Still Bind Them to You

As our kids pull away during this identity-building process, we may wonder if they value anything we have to offer. What we heard loud and clear, however, is that they desperately want us to provide values they can return to—and affirmation they can cling to in the midst of all the scary changes.

Tie #1: Kids secretly appreciate having a family heritage and values they can return to.

With all the dismantling of their parents' building blocks, we were surprised by what the teens said their castles would probably look like in the end. Take a look at the survey results for those kids who specifically said they wanted their own identity:

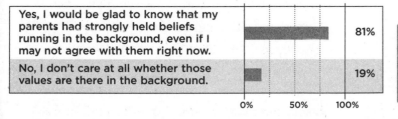

Although you want to find your own identity as a person and may be questioning your parents' values, would you be secretly glad if your family had positive, strongly expressed beliefs and values that you could return to If you wished? Choose one answer.

Yes, I would be glad to know that my parents had strongly held beliefs running in the background, even if I may not agree with them right now.	81%
No, I don't care at all whether those values are there in the background.	19%

0%   50%   100%

Identity

Even during the most intense time of questioning, more than eight out of ten kids say they absolutely do want to know that their parents have positive, strongly expressed beliefs and values that could be incorporated into their final sense of self. And among several cultural groups—especially Hispanics, African Americans, and those who regularly attend religious services—the number rose to near or above 90 percent.

 More than eight out of ten kids say they absolutely do want to know that their parents have positive, strongly expressed beliefs and values.

So many of the kids we talked to expressed a deep-seated pride in their family's heritage, traditions, and values:

- "My dad always says, 'The Johnson name stands for integrity.'"
- "My family says, 'The Reardons always defend the weak.'"
- "When my dad was teaching me about sex, he said, 'Our family always respects others, and we don't use other people's bodies for selfish purposes.'"
- "My family has a big Sabbath dinner on Friday nights, and all the relatives come over. Even though I sometimes resent missing the high-school football games, I have to admit that those dinners are important to me, and I'll probably carry on the tradition when I grow up."

But we also talked to many kids who didn't have those beliefs modeled for them and felt adrift:

- "My buddy's dad told him to do what he wanted to do and believe what he wanted to believe. It messed the guy up, and he couldn't wait to move out. He had no grounding, and he felt like he had to grow up on his own."
- "I couldn't find a reason to believe in God, but I see that my friends do. It makes me a little sad for my family. Maybe someday I'll believe."

As we listened to values-questioning kids expressing gratitude for their families' values, we realized that a strong sense of parental beliefs acts like a pole embedded in a rock—a pole to which the kids are tethered. Although they will probably explore in some turbulent directions, if they are firmly anchored, they're much less likely to get swept away.

Tie #2: Even kids who are pulling away want affirmation of who they are becoming.

As our kids navigate the inner and outer turmoil of these years, we often make the mistake of trying to assure them that we understand. "After all, I was a teenager once too," we observe. But the kids say that's no comfort. As one older teen explained, "When your kid declares, 'You just don't understand me!' what he's really saying is, 'I'm changing so much that I don't even understand *myself*, and it's scary. So I know that there's no way that someone else can possibly keep up.'"

One of the strongest trends we saw in our interviews and survey results was that as kids became their own people, they deeply wanted

Identity

their parents to recognize the changes taking place in their lives and to appreciate them as new and unique individuals. Because if they aren't a different person from the one you knew a few years ago, it means they haven't built their own castle yet. Look at our survey:

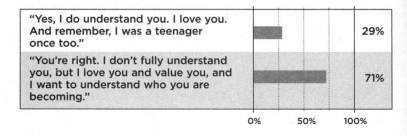

Imagine that you and your parents are having a conflict over something. You are angry or hurt that they just don't understand you. When you next talk face to face with your parents, which statement from them would most make you feel better? Choose one answer.

"Yes, I do understand you. I love you. And remember, I was a teenager once too."	29%
"You're right. I don't fully understand you, but I love you and value you, and I want to understand who you are becoming."	71%

Seven out of ten kids said that they would feel better if parents would simply acknowledge that they don't fully understand the changes going on in their kids and then affirm, "But I love you and value you, and I want to understand who you are becoming."

 Kids want their parents to recognize the changes, because if they aren't a different person, it means they haven't built their own castle yet.

One heartbreaking comment on the hunger for affirmation came from a high-school girl who overheard us talking one day in a coffee shop and told us of a pain that would probably be a total surprise to her parents:

> I have changed a lot this year, and I've pulled away from the quiet, kind of nerdy kid my mom was. I've become outgoing and even flirty. I'm careful with guys—I believe in waiting until marriage—but I'm really enjoying their interest. But my mom doesn't get me, and she seems to think I'm a slut. It kills me because she knows how she raised me and that I'm not going to go against such a core religious value and become a whore. I wish she knew the real me, but she just can't seem to get there. I just want her to like—or at least accept—the person I've become.

Rethinking Our Role

Although the identity-creating process is hard on our kids—and on us!—it also provides an opportunity for lifelong impact when we choose to guide their process of discovery rather than try to prevent it. If you're a Christian parent, you can make your child's identity search a high priority in your prayers. But you can also rest in the knowledge that the groundwork for who our kids will become has

Identity

been laid since early childhood and that God will be faithful to complete what he's been building in your child's life.

Beyond that, how else can we contribute positively to our kids' quest to know and become the individuals they're intended to be? Our research suggests three starting points:

1. Resist the urge to push.

This is one of the hardest and most critical things for a parent to do in the identity-questioning stage. Remember, your child has to dismantle your "components" before she knows whether or not she wants to keep them. So the harder you push your identity, beliefs, and opinions on her, the more urgently she'll feel compelled to distance herself from those specific things in order to become her own person.

Down, boy!

Many times, the teenagers told us that if parents would stifle the urge to impose their beliefs and instead relax a bit, they would feel *more* free to adopt those beliefs for themselves.

One reason teens consistently gave for shutting off communication is the belief that parents will "freak out" over what they say. So if you can force yourself to handle your child's curveballs calmly and without condemnation, he'll feel safe discussing his questions with you. It doesn't mean you have to leave him wondering what you think. It does mean resisting the urge to take it personally when he questions your building blocks.

I (Lisa) saw this in action just as we were starting this research. Our family has always believed that God answers the prayers of those who "earnestly seek him," as Psalms put it. One day when I encouraged one of my teenage daughters to pray about something that was bothering her, she sighed and said, "Mom, I'm just not sure that I believe like you do, that God really answers prayer."

Horrified, I nearly blurted out something like, "How can you *say* that?! You know God answers prayer! You've seen examples of that over and over!" It took everything within me to calmly answer, "Hmm… I see you're asking yourself some important questions. Why don't you journal about this to God and let me know what you come to on that, okay?"

 The harder you push your identity, beliefs, and opinions on her, the more urgently she'll feel compelled to distance herself from those specific things in order to become her own person.

Because of this research, I knew I couldn't push, nor could I compromise what I knew to be true. I needed to let her come to the truth for herself. And because I would sometimes find her in her room reading her Bible or journaling, I knew that she was truly

Identity

going through that process. I'm happy to report that just as we were putting the final touches on this book, she came home from church with tears in her eyes, saying, "Wow, you wouldn't believe how God answered prayer and spoke to me in the service this morning. He gave me insight about every major issue I'm dealing with right now."

After she worked through it for a year, what a joy it was to see her come to this realization on her own rather than simply accept it from me!

Lead by example.

As we saw in our survey, your kid probably craves the security of knowing that she is part of a family with a sense of heritage, faith, and strongly held positive values. So you'll want to watch for natural opportunities to articulate and live out those family priorities.

Although your kid would never be so uncool as to say so, he is watching your actions closely. And at least some of the stories and life experiences he shares with you ("This guy fudged on his time-card…") will provide opportunities for positive social reference if you're on the alert.

2. Strive to see and affirm the person your child is becoming.

As our kids formulate their identities, we can (and the kids say *should*) openly acknowledge that we don't necessarily understand them. As one teenage girl said to her parents, "I know you're really trying to understand what I'm going through, but it's okay that you can't totally relate. Just acknowledge that times have changed, and give me a hug when I'm stressed."

Guidance counselor Nerida Edwards says parents often tell her, "I feel like I don't know my child." Her response? "Well, they've changed a lot, and you probably don't. Take them to Waffle House or Starbucks for an hour, and leave both your cell phones at home. Do something they will enjoy, and in most cases they will talk to you if they know you really want to listen."

As simple as it might sound, one of the best ways to assure our child that we do want to understand her new identity is to actually investigate it. To move past your preconceptions, you might even pretend you're meeting your child for the first time. What would you notice and ask if you had the clear eyes of an outsider? Might you sense, for example, a previously unrecognized loneliness underneath the vivacious surface of your eighth-grader? What might you learn if you asked, "Do you feel included in this family? at your school?"

As you get to know the person your child is becoming, you may notice her hunger for appreciation. As part of her social referencing, she's wondering, *What do Mom and Dad think of who I'm becoming?* Look for ways to sincerely express your pride in the positive ways she's growing. As one girl said, "It would mean so much to me if,

Identity

instead of harping on me for always being on the go, my mom would say, 'Wow, you've really become an amazing, independent person who's not afraid to try new things.'"

Even when we can't help but notice their negative behaviors—especially the prickliness and defensiveness that so often accompany our children's inner confusion about who they are—they still need our encouragement and affection. Even though we sometimes feel that giving it is like hugging a porcupine!

> They still need our encouragement and affection. Even though we sometimes feel that giving it is like hugging a porcupine!

3. Gently point kids toward their core identity.

As our children look at the world and try to figure how they fit into it, they'll be tempted to concentrate on many surface, temporary things. Although we cannot push, we can gently open their eyes to thinking of themselves as children of God first and foremost.

Recently one of my (Lisa's) daughters was feeling frustrated. "I don't feel like I'm the best in anything," she said. "Not my sport, my music, my job, or my grades. I'm not a model Christian. It's like I don't have anything that is clearly *me*."

I decided to share something I'd once heard from pastor and author Mike Bickle. She watched as I drew a diagram: a little circle surrounded by a bigger one. I labeled various places around the outer circle with words like *appearance, talents, friends, school grades,* and so on, then asked her to mark the areas that were bothering her.

I said, "The labels in this outer ring are where many people look for their identity. But if so, God will allow pain in those areas to push us to this center circle, which is our core identity: that we are lovers of God, beloved of God, and we abide in the heart of a God who adores us. If we try to base our identity on any of these other aspects, we'll become frustrated—but we'll find contentment when we focus on our real identity."

My daughter stared at the paper for a minute. "Wow. That's exactly what I needed."

Identity Circle

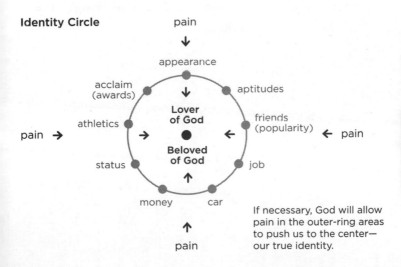

If necessary, God will allow pain in the outer-ring areas to push us to the center— our true identity.

Identity

"Train Up a Child in the Way He Should Go"

In a few short years, the angst of these teenage years will be a memory. And our kids will move from seeing us as embarrassing to recognizing our wisdom and wanting our friendship. Look at the perspective of these twenty-two-year-olds after only a few years of distance:

- "Now I think my parents are terrific, and I want to do what they did when I'm a parent. I would never have said that at sixteen."

- "I used to be embarrassed by my family. But now I love my family just the way it is: joyful, loud, stressful, sarcastic, screaming, loving, disorganized, always surprising people. I wouldn't change a thing."

Four

THE GOOD THING ABOUT
BEING THE BAD GUY

*Why your child secretly hopes
you'll stand your ground*

> Although our teens test our authority and
> argue with rules, they secretly want us to
> stand firm as parents and will lose respect
> for us if we don't.

One of my (Lisa's) favorite home-movie clips is of our daughter Hannah, at age four, spinning in her dad's big leather office chair and proclaiming, "My name is Hannah Rice, and I'm in charge of this house!" She then proceeds to list all the powers and privileges of being in charge.

The scene is amusing because it's cutely absurd. But in our

research, we got the uncomfortable sense that in a whole lot of households the kids are, in essence, the ones in charge.

A Parent, Not a Friend

In the last two chapters, we've seen how our kids' intense desire to do what they want and to find their own identity can result in challenging our authority at every step. Since they seem to want to be in charge of their own lives, parents who are exhausted by the battle may begin wonder if it's time to transition from being their child's authority figure to being a friend.

We must confess that as we began to investigate this question in our focus groups and kid-on-the-street interviews, we expected these highly independent teenagers to lobby hard for hands-off parenting. So we were quite surprised to hear that—almost without exception—the kids *don't want hands-off parenting*! Sure, they said they would grumble and fight—sometimes intensely—against parental discipline and boundaries. But deep down, they know they need a loving and firm adult to be in charge—a parent who doesn't use their authority to "show who's boss" but to train kids to be in charge of their own lives in just a few short years.

As one teen put it, "I have friends at school; I need parents!"

Think she's an exception to the rule? Take a look at what the survey takers said:

Most teenagers say that they want to grow up to be a good person. If you had to choose between two ways that your parents could relate to you, which one would you choose to help you become the good person you want to be? Choose one answer.

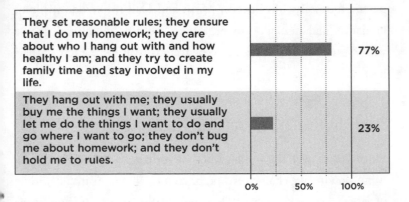

They set reasonable rules; they ensure that I do my homework; they care about who I hang out with and how healthy I am; and they try to create family time and stay involved in my life.	77%
They hang out with me; they usually buy me the things I want; they usually let me do the things I want to do and go where I want to go; they don't bug me about homework; and they don't hold me to rules.	23%

Even though teenagers do clamor for freedom, three out of four would *choose* for their parents to stay on top of them and not just let them do whatever they want with that freedom. Yes, you read that right: *as long as authority is exerted in order to help them develop their own capacity for responsibility,* the kids agree with the parenting books about the need for parents to take charge!

One insightful teen spoke for many when he confessed, "We haven't completely learned how to discipline ourselves yet, so we still need their discipline until we learn it for ourselves."

Taking Charge

"I have friends at school; I need parents!"

Although the kids we talked to think it's wonderful to have a close relationship with their parents, they said friendship should never be the primary goal. Instead, while they remain under their parents' authority, they expect Mom and Dad to provide wisdom, guidance, and discipline to help them become wonderful people whom their parents will *want* to be friends with for the rest of their lives.

The Truth About Taking Charge

Once you're over the initial shock of realizing your child actually wants you to take charge (except, of course, when he's in the middle of receiving your discipline!), let's look at the other surprising truths we learned about kids' views on parental authority.

Truth #1: Teens see your taking charge as a form of love and security.

Even when we know we need to take charge as parents, we sometimes feel uncomfortable exercising our authority—or we just get fed up with the resulting drama and tantrums. It often seems easier to simply let things go. But the teens we interviewed said it's our *job* to be the bad guy. And when parents sidestep that role, kids feel insecure and even uncared for.

They feel unsettled when parents aren't in control.

One teen described how he feels when his divorced parents often wrongly assume he's with the other parent: "Mom's always at her boyfriend's house, so I'm home alone. So I don't see a point in going home. At 12:30 a.m., I'm thinking I should call my mom, but then again, why should I? Sometimes I actually feel bad because there's no one who's asking me to call or come home at a certain time. It's kinda weird."

 The teens we interviewed said it's our *job* to be the bad guy.

Instead of being thrilled with this lack of supervision, he feels unsettled. Though we hope that specific situation is unusual, we heard many other comments that indicated uneasiness:

- "I can't believe my parents give me a curfew but don't enforce it. It makes me feel like they don't really care...like they've tuned me out for the night."
- "My dad isn't a father figure. He tries to be my friend more than my dad. So I can get anything out of him."

And there are different types of control.

Even if we're trying our best to take charge, we might miss some subtle ways kids try to seize the reins. I (Shaunti) saw a great example

Taking Charge

one day when a close friend tried to drop off her eleven-year-old son at a new summer day camp. He pitched a fit, crying, "I want to go to work with you!" Then he sat on the steps and refused to walk into the building. Although she was steaming mad, his worn-out single mom didn't want to make a scene, plus she was concerned about the level of upheaval in his life. So she took him to work.

Later, I described the scene for our consultant psychotherapist, Dr. Julie Carbery, who put her finger on the additional "Aha": my friend was letting her son control not just her actions but also her emotions. And although he probably got a rush from it at the time, his victory made his world less secure. As Dr. Carbery put it, he was looking to Mom to bring some order to the chaos of his life. Her response instead confirmed that he—an eleven-year-old boy—was really the one in control. And that knowledge probably made the inner chaos worse.

Thankfully, our friend ended up cracking down a lot more over the next six months, and we've seen her son become more respectful and pleasant to be around. He's turning into the kid he was meant to be.

Not that they'll ever tell you this...

You will probably never hear your kids admit within earshot that they appreciate your discipline. So when you hear complaining instead, remember these words from one representative boy:

Yeah, I slam the door when I'm punished, and I'll mutter something under my breath. I'm mad at the moment, but I know even then that they're doing it for me and for my good.

Look at how kids responded when we painted a common scenario on the survey.

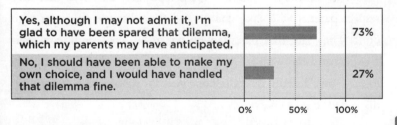

Imagine this scenario: Your parents don't allow you to go to a concert wIth kids they suspect drink a lot, and you are furious. But later you find that everyone was drinking and driving home drunk. If you had been there, you would have had to make an uncomfortable choice between seeming uncool by refusing to get in the car, or riding with a drunk driver. Looking back, are you glad your parents made you stay home? Choose one answer.

Yes, although I may not admit it, I'm glad to have been spared that dilemma, which my parents may have anticipated.	73%
No, I should have been able to make my own choice, and I would have handled that dilemma fine.	27%

0%   50%   100%

Again, three out of four kids would secretly be glad (later!) that Mom or Dad suspected a risky situation and cracked down.

Taking Charge

Interestingly, that answer earned a 100-percent unanimous response among teens attending private Protestant or Jewish schools.

"Love makes decisions in the best interest of the kid, no matter how much the kid kicks and screams."

One astute high-school sophomore summarized the perspective of many teens (and parents): "Love makes decisions in the best interest of the kid, no matter how much the kid kicks and screams."

Truth #2: If you aren't in charge, your kids will lose respect for you and discount your authority.

Loose parenting isn't cool.

In our interviews and surveys, teens repeatedly admitted that they respect parents who take charge and they disrespect parents who don't. They said that parents who try to be "cool" and earn their child's friendship with an "anything goes" approach are more likely to earn their disdain. And the same goes for parents who are just too distracted to take charge.

Teens repeatedly admitted that they respect parents who take charge and they disrespect parents who don't.

With even these few comments, we think you'll see how loose parenting affects a child's respect level:

- "Parents always give in. They say, 'You're grounded,' and then they forget, and we kids don't take them seriously. We laugh behind their backs."

- "Parents these days have checked out. They're too busy, and they're just hoping things will work out okay without them. I hope I'm not like that as a dad."

- "My mom and dad are kind of stupid about the whole parenting thing. It wasn't modeled for them, and they have no idea how to give us any kind of consistency with rules or punishments. It's kind of all-or-nothing."

It's painful to imagine how many parents are misguidedly trying to build a relationship with their children by being a bit lax and are instead ruining the relationship.

Let's not pick a fight.

Of course, some parents aren't trying to be cool; they just don't want to ruin their precious, limited time with their kids. This exchange from one focus group shows the flaw in that approach:

> *Teen 1:* "A lot of dads back off more because they're not home a lot, so they don't want to be the bad guy when they *are* home, and they let the rules slide. It's like, 'I'm only home a little, so let's not pick a fight.'"

Taking Charge

Teen 2: "But if they're there in the house, but not there as a parent should be, they still aren't *there,* really. And if the dad *will* pick a fight when he needs to, I bet he'll have to do it a lot less often."

When parents don't give in.

Of course, plenty of parents hold firmly to the reins of authority. One college student explained how his parents' willingness to pick a fight transformed his teen defiance:

> Did you ever say, "So?" when your parents told you were grounded? And then they added a week, and you still said, "So?" And then they added a month, and you said, "So?" You only do that once in your life.

 "They didn't want the fake mom who was trying too hard to be cool. And they actually loved the fact that they had to abide by the rules."

Another older teen offered the surprising revelation that a little old-fashioned discipline can actually *raise* a parent's Cool Quotient:

> When I was in high school, Mom never tried to be cool. She actually yelled at my friends because they were being

stupid, and they liked it! They didn't want the fake mom who was trying too hard to be cool. And they actually loved the fact that they had to abide by the rules.

Truth #3: Even "good kids" need watchful attention and discipline.

Another reason we may not be taking charge is that we simply don't think we need to. So many kids look good on the outside—and may even be responsible in most cases. But as we discovered, even good kids sometimes make really bad choices.

I (Lisa) was forcibly confronted with this fact during a focus group with some older teens. When I asked if they ever did stupid things that they regretted later, they told a hair-raising tale of their exploits just the night before:

> *Boy 1:* "We were in my brother's tricked-out Integra, heading to Whataburger. There were all these cop cars around, and we got freaked because we'd been smoking a little pot. So we turned off into a neighborhood and waited, then headed back toward the fast-food place. But around the next turn, we saw a cop on the side of the road coming closer. We panicked, turned around, floored it, and ran a red light to get away. The cop turned his lights on and followed us, but we lost him. We were going like a hundred and forty miles per hour. The brakes were

smoking. We thought it was pretty funny at the time, but
this morning we said how that was all pretty stupid."

I tried to keep a straight face at that last statement and just nod-
ded. Then, not ten minutes later, this same young man complained
that his mother didn't trust him enough!

> *Boy 1:* "I feel not trusted sometimes. My mom is so
> needlessly strict with my curfew."
>
> *Boy 2:* "We're not really bad. All we do is hang out at the
> burger place and play video games. They don't need to worry."
>
> *Boy 3:* "Yeah, we're responsible, good kids."

I finally said, "Um…you just told me you outran a cop last
night—while you were high on pot. How can you say you're good
kids?"

> *Boy 1* (seeming truly puzzled): "But we *are* good. We're
> not on drugs or in jail…and we're not, like, tattoo freaks
> or anything."

What the "good kids" are doing.

As we saw in the chapter on freedom, such downplaying and ration-
alization are very common. On the survey, we found that almost all
kids see themselves as good—even when their behavior isn't.

Do you consider yourself a good kid? Choose one answer.

Yes	93%
No	7%

0%   50%   100%

An amazing 93 percent said they were "good kids." Hmm…

We guessed they meant that they weren't doing things that they shouldn't do. We'd also heard enough spine-chilling stories to guess that the kids might be deluding themselves. So we investigated further, conducting (on the advice of our survey expert) a written follow-up survey of one hundred anonymous teens at shopping malls in different cities. The teens answered the "good kid" question (among others) and also checked off how many times, if ever, they had done certain things teenagers probably shouldn't be doing.

Nearly all the kids admitted to doing several stupid things at least once. Lying was, unfortunately, nearly universal, and cheating was pretty close. But of those who identified themselves as "good kids," 46 percent also confessed to having done more than just experiment with trouble.

Specifically, that 46-percent group admitted to committing one or more of the following offenses three or more times: drinking, using drugs (pot and/or harder drugs), wild partying, sneaking out, having sexual intercourse or oral sex, stealing, or driving at scary speeds (more than forty miles per hour *above* the speed limit), among other things.

Taking Charge

Wake up!

Thankfully, if they're being honest, roughly half of all "good kids" are abstaining from multiple infractions of the worst offenses. But since half aren't, we need to be watchful. It's time to wake up to the fact that our own children may be numbered among the good kids experimenting with trouble.

Please hear us: when we identify negative behaviors common among teens today, we are *not* implying that parents should accept them simply because they're so widespread. We do, however, strongly believe that as we get wise to the reality of what's "normal" in our kids' world, we'll be more prepared to help them choose a much better path.

Unfortunately, middle-school guidance counselor Nerida Edwards says she's saddened by "the sheer number of parents who simply don't want to hear or believe bad things about their children." Well, those children themselves are advising parents to open their eyes:

- "Parents are very much in the dark, and they're not trying too hard to see, either."
- "My parents would have a heart attack if they could see the things I do when they're not around."
- "Parents are so clueless sometimes. My friend Tiffany's mom thinks her daughter is an angel just because she's a cute, friendly cheerleader with a swinging blonde ponytail.

What they don't see is that Tiffany can drink all her girl-friends under the table."

- "I work in a Christian bookstore after school, and one parent came in and was upset that the teen study Bible we sold talked about sexual issues. I'm thinking, *Oh, lady, you just don't have a clue, do you?*"

And as one teenager wishes she could tell parents:

- "You have to be involved in your kids' lives and not be oblivious!"

 "You have to be involved in your kids' lives and not be oblivious!"

Truth #4: Kids appreciate rules more when they understand the reason behind them.

As kids explained their respect for parents who take charge, there was one clear caveat: parents have to be willing to explain *why* the rules and boundaries exist and not appear arbitrary, so that the teens can understand the reasons for themselves. One teen observed in her focus group, " 'Because I said so' only works on very young children."

As another teen gratefully observed: "My parents take time to tell the reasons for the rules, and we discuss it if I really disagree with them. It makes me feel respected to be included in these discussions and to understand why they do what they do with us."

Taking Charge

On the other hand, kids who don't get the reason for the rule seem convinced their parents are trying to "control me for no reason," as these comments show:

- "My parents think it's easier to just come up with random rules that they throw at me *to keep me under their thumb.* If I question them, they get irritated. They don't want to have to turn off the TV and actually think about and discuss why they made up these rules" (emphasis ours).

Kids who don't get the reason for the rule seem convinced their parents are trying to "control me for no reason."

- "If they can't think of a reason, they'll just say no. My friend Brad lives next to Wal-Mart, and we all hang out there. But then Mom found out and said no, and when I asked why, she tried to make up a reason. 'You'll get killed.' 'Really, Mom? I'll get killed at Brad's or killed at Wal-Mart?'"

Are You Ready to Rumble?

So what does it mean, in practice, to be involved authority figures who aren't oblivious? And is it possible to maintain discipline without fighting our freedom-seeking kids every step of the way? Thankfully, the kids we interviewed provided great insights for how to communicate and take charge in a way that they can respect, and that will hopefully lessen those inevitable clashes of will.

1. Purposefully pull on the velvet gloves of authority.

Many of us so often run from one parenting fire to the next that we never truly get out in front of the process. But it actually *reduces* the overall stress when parents spend the extra effort to proactively implement an improved "take-charge plan."

Through a nonparenting experience, I (Shaunti) recently saw what a huge difference a take-charge plan makes. When *For Women Only* became a surprise bestseller, my life suddenly became extremely chaotic, as success bred more opportunities and demands than I could handle. Because I hated saying no and disappointing people, I soon became exhausted, started missing deadlines, and disappointed people anyway! So I hired one of Lisa's no-nonsense friends, Linda, to be my project manager—essentially, to be the "parent" whose job it is to make sure I'm doing a good job. She's quite comfortable saying no, and we tease her that her motto about taking charge is, "Put on your big girl panties and deal with it!"

As parents, some of us may need to adopt a similar motto to get over any squeamishness about taking charge, and to remind ourselves that we don't need to apologize for asserting our authority.

Taking Charge

However, as we'll see in the next chapter, we want to exercise our authority in ways that build our kids up and nurture a sense of personal responsibility. Despite our (and their) most valiant efforts, our kids will still make mistakes. And whether or not consequences are appropriate in those cases, we need to demonstrate understanding, compassion, and a desire to help them learn from those mistakes.

 We want to exercise our authority in ways that build our kids up and nurture a sense of personal responsibility.

2. Establish clear rules—and help your kid "own" them.

As noted, we need to explain the "why" behind our boundaries and decisions.* But we can't stop there: we need to help our kids "own" those reasons for themselves.

One college kid advised, "Parents should teach 'wrong versus wise,' not 'wrong versus right.'" When our teens come to us with a request, what if we don't jump right in with the answer but instead prompt them to think it through? We can help them consider

---

*   One caveat: experts note that in families where the kids have never learned how to respect authority, parents may need to teach "absolute authority" first and require the teen to defer simply out of respect for the parents' role as head of the family. We suggest such families enlist a family therapist to help.

whether something is wise by encouraging them to ask themselves such tough questions as, "Does this friend or activity have the potential to trip me up?"

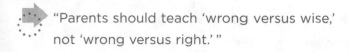

"Parents should teach 'wrong versus wise,' not 'wrong versus right.'"

In addition, some kids (and their parents) suggested bringing kids in on the process of setting the rules and consequences up front. For example, in the Edwards home, before the children could enjoy certain privileges, they had to come up with a list of rules that they agreed to abide by—and that their parents could agree with. For example, "If my parents ever catch me driving friends who aren't wearing seat belts, I'll lose the privilege of driving friends."

3. Forget "one size fits all."

Just as a good salesman doesn't treat all customers the same but tailors plans to their individual needs, so you'll want to tailor your parenting strategy to sell your child on the fact that you are treating him as an individual. As one teen advised, "Know your kid's character. If he does drugs, clamp down! If he makes good choices, lighten up!"

The principle of tailor-made parenting also applies to consequences, especially now that we know that certain freedoms—and loss of them—mean more to some kids than others. One teen confessed, "Grounding is torturous, but it works on me." But another older teen blew the cover on a lot of her younger peers with this comment:

> If I was sent to my room, I'd act all upset, but it was
> totally fake. My room was a safe haven, and we *want* to
> be cut off from the family and the conflict. That's not the
> answer. The answer for a teen is heavy chores...a big,
> horrible list of heavy chores.

4. Expect emotionalism and testing—and remain calm.

As you have no doubt noticed, our kids *will* test us to see whether we'll take charge and enforce boundaries. Our children are asking themselves, *Is Dad really going to hold the line on my curfew? Am I going to be able to get Mom all upset, or is she going to remain in control and stay calm even when I'm feeling out of control?*

Our kids *will* test us to see whether we'll take charge and enforce boundaries. They're asking, *Am I going to be able to get Mom all upset, or is she going to remain in control?*

And sometimes that testing will include dramatic, anger-filled protests, requiring even more determination on our part to remain calm and steadfast. We repeatedly tried to get the teenagers to tell us what punishment *wouldn't* make a kid upset, but no magic bullet emerged. Finally, one kid said it all: "There is no punishment a parent could give that wouldn't make a teenager feel rebellious and angry. It's just what you do when you're punished. You feel rebellious."

We need to be okay with the fact that if we do our job right, our kids will sometimes be angry with us. As my (Lisa's) husband, Eric, recently told our household of grounded and steaming-mad teens, "My job is not to produce happy teens; it's to produce well-adjusted, responsible adults."

5. Be their watchdog.

Because even good kids are sometimes caught up in situations beyond their control or are tempted to do foolish things, we simply need to be aware of where our kids are and what they're doing. It's also helpful to keep an ear to the ground by consulting with other parents: "This is Lisa, Hannah's mom. Hannah says they're going to McDonald's and then buzzing over to the mall. Is that what you're hearing?"

Your kid may—okay, *will*—accuse you of spying, but you can clarify that you're just filling the role of bodyguard, protecting her from things that neither you nor she wants to harm her. And when her resentment pours over, just repeat under your breath, "She'll thank me in five years, she'll thank me in five years…"

Taking Charge

6. And don't get drawn in to the "You don't trust me" debate.

The job of a Secret Service agent isn't to trust or distrust the person in his charge; it's to watch over and protect him, regardless.

To plaintive cries of "You don't trust me," we can answer something like this: "Whether I trust you has nothing to do with it. I do trust you to want to do the right thing, but I'm going to check up on you anyway. Because I certainly don't trust everyone else, and I don't know whether I can always trust the teen-hormone version of you. But regardless, protecting you is simply part of my job."

Take the Chair: They'll Thank You Later!

Taking charge in a firm and loving way can feel daunting when our kids seem to be resisting us at every turn. If you're like most parents we've met in our travels, you're willing—and trying—to exercise your authority; you just need reassurance that continuing to stand firm is the right thing to do.

 Literally hundreds of teens said they might resist their parents' rules now but will probably want to parent their own children in exactly the same way.

We encourage you to take heart in the literally hundreds of teens who said they might resist their parents' rules now but will probably want to parent their own children in exactly the same way. Consider what one survey-taker wrote when asked what he'd like to tell his dad:

> I'm sorry for not always doing my chores, and I know I should have helped out more, but I just made some bad choices. But you have raised me so well, and I now know all of my limitations, and I am so grateful to have had a parent like you. You have helped me realize what kind of person I want to be in the future and what kind of dad I want to be to my kids someday.

We believe that you, too, will enjoy the results as you calmly take your rightful seat in the big executive chair, saying, "I am the parent, and *I* am in charge of this house."

Taking Charge

Five

I WILL BE HERE FOR YOU

How to help teens feel secure in the ascent to adulthood, even when they lose their footing

Although they may not look like it, kids want the security of knowing we are making the effort to understand them and will be there for them regardless of their mistakes—but kids will emotionally shut out a parent they see as judgmental.

Once upon a time, the parable goes, an impatient young man demanded his share of his inheritance while his father was still living. He then moved to a distant country and promptly blew his father's hard-earned fortune with wild living. When a famine left him near starvation and even pig food started to look appealing, he decided to throw himself on his father's mercy.

The wayward son limped toward home, bowed by shame and failure. Picture his shock when he saw his distinguished father shunning all concern about his appearance and *running* to meet him. Imagine how the young man, who was expecting humiliation, felt when his father threw a beautiful robe around his dirty shoulders and shouted with joy that his son had been found!

Have you considered how this story might have ended if you or I were the parent of that young scalawag? Certainly we'd want to inform the returning son of our disappointment in his behavior and give him, at a minimum, a good talking-to. And would we have even let him take his inheritance in the first place?

Are we willing to let our children make some mistakes, or to consider that the cost of those mistakes may be worth it because of the maturity it will bring? When our kids rebel or fail, what might they expect from us? Disappointment and shame? Or understanding, unconditional love, and security?

"Will You Be There When I Need You?"

In the last chapter, we discussed that our children need to see us taking charge. But as we do, our children also desperately need to see that we will be there for them no matter what.

As parents, we often feel as if our kids view us as a necessary evil, as tyrants they can't wait to escape. But don't be fooled. Our kids care deeply about their relationship with us, and they need to know that our love and support are secure.

Our research showed that if we resolutely demonstrate that fact, regardless of the bumps in the road, our children will open up to us as much as words-challenged teens possibly can. But—and this is the hard part to hear—if time after time they feel judged or abandoned, they're extremely likely to shut us out emotionally.

Here's the scenario we offered the kids:

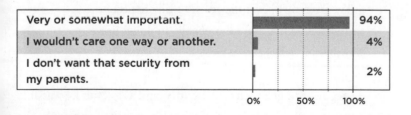

Suppose you could wave a magic wand and start over again with your parents, where neither they nor you had ever made mistakes with each other. How important is it to you to have the security of knowing your parents will always be there for you and that they at least make the effort to understand your world? Choose one answer.

Very or somewhat important.	94%
I wouldn't care one way or another.	4%
I don't want that security from my parents.	2%

0%   50%   100%

Security

If starting from a clean slate (in other words, eliminating the possibility that the kids had already shut their parents out), 94 percent of them said they needed the security of *knowing* that an understanding parent would always be there for them.

 "I need my parents. I need their assurance, their backup, their support. Because they've been there, I can talk with them about anything."

The teens we talked to repeatedly stressed the importance of what we might call "unconditional security." Look at one teenage boy's description of his parents:

> No matter when and where, if I was intoxicated, they
> would come—any time, anywhere. It reminds me that
> I need this… I need my parents. I need their assurance,
> their backup, their support. Because they've been there,
> I can talk with them about anything. And as much grief
> as I've given them over the years, I really respect how
> they've treated me, and I'll probably do things just the
> way they did when I have kids.

This guy felt a great sense of security, and as a result he was able to maintain a good relationship with his parents even when he messed up and they cracked down. Regrettably, we also heard many sober warnings about what happens when kids feel they *don't* have that security. A girl we talked to in a shopping mall explained why she has shut her mom out:

> After my parents divorced, my mom saw me spreading
> my wings and changing, and she freaked out. She criti-
> cized me so much without ever really trying to know
> me that after a while I stopped caring what she thought.
> I still care about what Dad thinks, but my mom could
> tell me I'm the biggest slut and I'd say, "That's fine,"
> because I've locked her out of my heart and life.

Providing Unconditional Security

As we talked to the kids, we heard some immensely valuable advice on how parents can be firm in discipline without *ever* implying that our love and support are conditional— a conclusion they jump to far more quickly than we may have realized.

Our publisher's Colorado Springs office overlooks a majestic sweep of the Rocky Mountains, where rock climbing is a favorite sport. One of the most vital skills of safe rock climbing is called belaying, which offers a fascinating picture of what it looks like when we create security our child can recognize and depend on. The word *belay* comes from a French verb meaning "to hold fast," and the belayer's job is to protect a climber by making sure the rope holds fast in the event of a fall. With some simple techniques, a belayer can hold the entire weight of a falling climber, ensure she doesn't fall too far, and carefully guide her to a safe spot where she can resume climbing.

Just like a climber navigating a sheer cliff, your child knows perfectly well that he might slip as he ventures up the rock face of his life. He needs to know that because you're there, he won't fall far emotionally. In moving toward adulthood, he has to do the exhilarating but scary climbing himself, but as he does, several key things will assure him that you are vigilantly watching him make his way and that you're holding his rope securely.

Assurance #1: Kids want to know you'll make the effort to understand them and be part of their world.

As we've seen, during their search for identity our kids find comfort in knowing that we're trying to keep up as best we can. Here's how one insightful girl described what she needs from her parents during this bewildering time:

> Being a teenager is like trying to run down an up escalator. It's going up, whether you want to or not. And you've got all these battles going on, all the time. Externally, it's stuff like school, popularity, and homework, but internally, it's about whether anyone understands you. And you can't really describe the heartbreak of trying to get your parents to notice and understand you.

I'm sure most parents do notice their kids, but often it doesn't look like it. Being on that up escalator is exciting, confusing, and risky, all at the same time. You constantly want to know what your parents think, but you constantly want to do it on your own, too. And parents are so far removed from their own adolescence that they just don't remember, so the kid has to sort of figure it out on her own, and that's scary.

As many kids pointed out, how can your child be assured that you'll "be there" for him if you don't even know him? The key, they said, is demonstrating that you *want* to know and understand him.

Your physical presence isn't enough.

Few parents would argue with the need to be present for their children, but according to both the teens and the licensed experts we talked to, many of us need to reconsider our understanding of what that really means. As one older teenager noted:

> Parents are too busy these days. They're always gone or are occupied with their personal desires and agendas. When kids need parents to push a bit to get inside, the parents don't because they're busy. Parents say, "Oh, they're okay. They look okay, so they must be okay." But often we're not.

Security

Many kids talked about how their mom or dad might be physically present yet so distracted by other things that "it feels like they've tuned me out and don't care about me." As I (Shaunti) listened to these kids describe the pain of being ignored, I felt utterly convicted.

I'd fallen into the habit of picking my kids up from school, then taking them to a park or playground—all the while continuing to make and take calls on my cell phone. I didn't even think they noticed that half the time I was driving or pushing them on the swings, I was simultaneously chatting away on my Bluetooth earpiece. Then my three-year-old started plaintively saying, "Mommy, take your ears off." And as a result of talking to the teenagers at the mall (and some challenging words from my husband!), I finally realized that *all* kids notice whether we're truly focusing on them and whether we're setting aside even legitimate distractions for a time.

 Kids notice whether we're truly focusing on them and whether we're setting aside even legitimate distractions for a time.

One girl drew gasps of longing from the other girls in her focus group when she described how her mom handled an "interruption" of her workday. She'd gone to her mother's home office to talk about a problem, then suddenly realized that she was making her mom late to a meeting. Chagrined, she gasped, "Mom, wait—don't you have to be somewhere?" And the mom leaned forward and said, "Honey, *you* are my most important place to be."

Enrolling in cross-cultural studies.

Most parents of teenagers feel as if they've been transported to a strange land, full of unknown tongues, outlandish customs, and un-fathomable traditions. Well, as one teen crisply put it, "Back at ya." They see us as foreigners too. And since they've spent plenty of time in "adult world," it sends a powerful message when we make an effort to understand theirs. In fact, the kids say this is one of the most effective ways parents can demonstrate that we truly care.

 Spending time in their world is one of the most effective ways to demonstrate that we care.

Vicki Courtney, author of *Your Girl* and *Your Boy*, shared a terrific story about "cross-cultural communication" between her husband, Keith, and their then-fifteen-year-old daughter, Paige:

Keith worried that the little girl who used to play board games with him was pulling away. As we talked about it, we realized we couldn't do anything about the fact that she had to separate herself from us. But that didn't mean we couldn't follow!

He wanted to demonstrate—in a way she would appreciate—that he still wanted a connection with her. So he started sending Paige regular little text messages on her cell phone, telling her that he loved her and was proud of her. He told me that he sometimes felt silly at first, but he kept it up, even though sometimes she didn't text back.

A few weeks later, I was driving Paige and her friends home from school when I heard a text chime from one of their phones. Paige's friends asked, "Who was that?"

"It's my dad," she responded. "He does that some-times, just to say hi."

Her friends started exclaiming, "Oh, that's so sweet!" "Oh, I wish my dad would do that!"

When I overheard Paige say, "Yeah. It's cool," I knew my husband had succeeded in getting into her world.

As this father understood, even simple efforts at immersing our-selves in "kid world" carry a huge emotional impact. We heard this echoed by countless kids, including this cute comment: "My parents were there for baseball games, and they came to all my concerts and band recitals. Even when my band performed at Eddie's Attic, they came—even though it *really* wasn't their thing!"

Assurance #2: Kids want you to be vulnerable and admit your mistakes.

It might seem that acting like "we know best" would create security in a kid, but ironically, as the kids get older, we found it's actually the opposite. We were quite taken aback as we heard that the teens feel *more* secure when their parents are vulnerable and willing to admit mistakes.

We were sitting in a coffee shop in the process of pondering why this might be true when a mother and teen daughter walked in. So we decided to ask the daughter that question. Her answer? "It absolutely makes me feel safer to know that Mom sees she did something to hurt me. If Mom is wrong and doesn't see it, I don't feel safe because I worry she'll just do it again."

Her mom chimed in: "I try to tell her, 'Please forgive me. God is the only perfect parent.' It makes it much easier for her to forgive me. It's hard to forgive someone who thinks she's right. I need to learn to see it through her eyes and say, 'Oh, wow, I actually was wrong.'"

Similarly, many teens said it built their confidence when parents could back down or change their minds when the kids made a good point. They didn't seem to be looking for an occasion to gloat, but viewed their parents' vulnerability as a way of bonding. One teen explained, "When parents say they were wrong, it's such a real connection. When my dad says, 'I shouldn't have handled it that way, Son,' I can respect him as a person."

If admitting mistakes builds security, then not admitting them clearly tears it down. As one teen put it, "My dad cannot say, 'I was wrong.' It's sad. And it drives a wedge."

FIGHTING FOR A SHAKY MARRIAGE

We know this may be difficult for some readers, but because so many kids raised the issue of how divorce affects security, we at least want to touch on it. Many kids said that although family discord was hard to deal with, the emotional and physical ramifications of divorce were harder. And even more found great security in knowing that Mom and Dad were fighting for their marriage and committed to making it work.

Here is how just one teen described the emotional instability of divorce: "It kind of messed me up when my parents divorced. I thought it was my fault. It made my whole world shaky, even as a little

Assurance #3: Kids want to know you'll be there for them, regardless of their mistakes.

Even if you provide the other elements of security, the kids said your efforts will probably be cancelled out if your child believes that when

kid. If I couldn't trust my parents to keep their promises to each other, what else couldn't I trust?"

None of us can change the past, but the kids did recommend that parents who were already divorced look for ways to fill in the "security gaps" for their kids. (Check out www.forparentsonly book.com for a list of helpful resources.)

And if you're working through conflict in your marriage or striving to keep a healthy one stable, you may be encouraged by this girl's words: "I'm only fifteen, but I know that having two parents who love each other and are committed to each other is my greatest treasure...I'm far richer than my best friend who lives in a country club and has divorced parents."

she messes up, you judge her or are "not there for her" (that is, if she perceives you to be withdrawing your love and support) just when she needs it most.

Even more distressing, a child who doesn't feel secure in her parents' love may eventually erect a "no trespassing" fence around her heart, shut herself off emotionally, and limit any relationship with Mom or Dad from that point forward, possibly even into adulthood. Look at this revealing exchange from one focus group:

Teen 1: "I can't tell my parents anything. I can't trust them. I tell my friends."

Teen 2: "But my friends haven't gone through the stuff my parents have. So it would be good to be able to talk to them. We're just scared of their reaction."

Teen 3: "If the reaction is always bad, you'll lose the whole communication thing with your parents and turn to your friends. Your friends understand you. The problem is that forty years later, those kids still aren't communicating with their parents."

 A child who doesn't feel secure in her parents' love may eventually erect a "no trespassing" fence around her heart.

Thankfully, most kids we talked to said they believed their parents were at least trying to be supportive. However, there unfortunately were a few who perceived their parents as judgmental and even intolerant of mistakes. In most of those cases, the kids said they'd already shut out their parents emotionally, and sometimes, they said, irreparably. Look at the survey results.

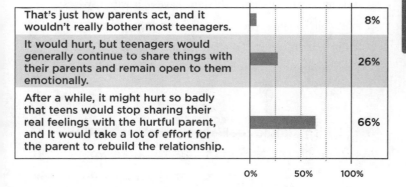

In your experience, when teenagers have made mistakes, how do they respond when they feel their parents judge them harshly or are not there for them when they most need them? Choose one answer.

That's just how parents act, and it wouldn't really bother most teenagers.	8%
It would hurt, but teenagers would generally continue to share things with their parents and remain open to them emotionally.	26%
After a while, it might hurt so badly that teens would stop sharing their real feelings with the hurtful parent, and it would take a lot of effort for the parent to rebuild the relationship.	66%

0%   50%   100%

In *For Men Only: A Straightforward Guide to the Inner Lives of Women,* my (Shaunti's) husband, Jeff, and I show men that most wives don't feel permanently loved once they get married. Even secure women deal with an underlying "Does he really love me?" insecurity and need frequent reassurance, especially in the face of conflict.

Well, our research revealed that our kids *need that same reassurance.* They need to see that Mom and Dad will stand by them, support them, love them, and help them even if they've made a terrible mistake. And if they don't see that, something in them seems to assume that Mom and Dad's love is conditional. This pain-filled comment is representative of what we heard from quite a few teens:

> I wish I could really know that, no matter what stupid
> thing I did, my parents would be there to hear me out
> and support me. I definitely don't have that with my
> mom. She's happy when I'm good and angry when
> I'm bad. It's like there's no area for mistakes or realness.
> Their approval of me is based solely on how well I'm
> doing.

 "I wish I could really know that, no matter what stupid thing I did, my parents would be there to hear me out and support me."

Building Trust That Lasts a Lifetime

Thankfully, we heard lots of encouraging stories about parents who weren't handling mistakes perfectly but were trying. And that effort to be loving and accepting even while challenging them to do better spoke volumes to the kids—and in the long run also seemed to be more productive.

Consider this story from a teen who came face to face with evidence of her dad's deep love:

> When I was seventeen I snuck out the window to be
> with my boyfriend. My parents found out and came
> and found me. I was so embarrassed and ashamed,
> but my dad sat down with me and told me that I had
> probably forgotten how valuable I was and that God
> had a great husband for me that I should save myself for.
> I was grounded from seeing the guy, but I came away
> from the situation knowing how much I was loved and
> valued no matter what.

When our kids see that even when they disappoint us we will be there backing them up, loving them, and desiring the best for them, they are much more likely to feel open toward us for years to come. Yes, some serious situations (beyond the scope of this book) may require "tough love" and the guidance of a professional family counselor. But in general, since most kids recognize when they've disappointed their parents, assuring kids of our unconditional support has a major impact.

So what are some tangible ways to ensure that your child feels

Security

unconditionally secure? Here are a few suggestions from the teens themselves:

1. Show you're interested in the day-to-day stuff.

Sometimes we think that because our kids don't *offer* to tell us things as much anymore, that they *won't*, but that isn't usually true—as long as we let them know we are available and interested. It might be enlightening to ask your child what makes you seem available or unavailable!

No matter how much or how little your child chooses to share, your effort to be present, both physically and emotionally, sends an important message. As one teen suggested, "Ask one question a day. Show that you're interested in the day-to-day stuff your kids are doing. It shows you care."

Find the places and activities that help your *child open up.*

One day, I (Shaunti) was sharing with a friend my concern about not letting my travel schedule keep me away from the kids too much while they are small. She raised an eyebrow and said, "You know it'll be even more important to be intentional when they're older, right?" She then made a perceptive point: "When kids are six and hurt themselves, ice cream can fix it. But when they're older and hurt, ice cream doesn't fix things anymore. It takes much more time and effort to tune in to their problems; you need to get totally committed to real, personal involvement in their day-to-day activities and attitudes. Because that is when they'll open up to you."

Since every kid is different, you'll want to look for the environment or venue that will help *your* child feel comfortable opening up. One girl echoed the adage about "location, location, location" when she said, "I don't talk to my mom at home because there are too many people and distractions, but when we drive around together, that's when I talk."

Or look at this older teen guy's remark: "I share myself in my writing, and my dad used to read all of it. He kinda stopped in high school, and I really missed that connection. When I was trying to find myself, it would have been great for him to use that as a springboard to talk about who I was, who I'd become."

 Your effort to be present, both physically and emotionally, sends an important message.

Like the dad who took up text messaging to stay in touch with his daughter, you may need to venture into your child's world in search of ways to underscore your interest. Go ahead and ask your child for suggestions—then be sure to follow through. And unless he explicitly says otherwise, assume that he values your presence and interest in his activities, even if he never says so.

2. Respond to mistakes with reassurances of your love and support.

Just as we need those close to us to offer grace when we make mistakes, our kids need us to recognize that they will blow it once in a while. As one teen put it: "The sooner that parents realize kids will make mistakes and meet them in the middle, the better." In teen-speak, that means parents should include compassion and calmness along with consequences.

Look at this example from a college-age guy:

> My parents picked me up at a party when I was sixteen and wasted. They just came and got me. Dad made me cut the grass at eight the next morning. He had understanding, but he had consequences, too. He said, "From now on, you're gonna call me, and we want the whens and wheres." And now I respect that.

Be calm.

As that example implies, we need to determine in advance to handle our kids' mistakes calmly—even taking time if we need it to cool down. Perhaps because their own emotions are so chaotic, the kids repeatedly told us that when their parents responded emotionally, it undermined the kids' sense of security and willingness to be open in the future. As one said, "I feel like my parents are out of control when there's yelling."

For a crash course in how your child perceives your reactions, ask her for an example of when she perceived you as overreacting. Then ask, "How could I have handled it better, yet in a way that still allowed you to learn from the consequences of your actions?"

"Tell me you're on my side."

Especially in the majority of cases where kids *know* they've messed up, along with their consequences they need a double or triple serving of reassurance that you love them and will be there for them. One teen said, "I'd just like to hear that my parents understand me and love me, no matter what I just told them."

Another suggested, "Tell them, 'I'm on your side. You're safe. There are still consequences, but you're safe, and I'm going to support you. We'll work through this with you.'"

"Tell them, 'I'm on your side.... There are still consequences, but you're safe, and I'm going to support you.'"

Kids also need to hear, "I forgive you." That may not come easily on the heels of some confessions, but it helps to remember just how much God has forgiven us. After one daughter got in trouble, her mom said, "You've gone against our values and have hurt the trust between us, but I forgive you. How could I not, after God has forgiven me for everything I've done?"

Security

"I know you want to do the right thing."

As we teach our kids about moral issues, we also want to carefully avoid accusing them of bad heart-motives—or any comments or actions that might lead our kids to *think* we're doing so. As essential as it is to say, "This thing you did was very wrong," it's just as crucial to make sure they know that we're *not* silently finishing the sentence with, *and I think you're a bad person.* As one kid noted, "It is absolutely imperative for parents to affirm their kids like, 'I know you want to do the right thing.'"

It's apparently quite easy to trip into shaming our kids for their mistakes without realizing it. We heard from quite a few hurting kids who are convinced their parents are judging their hearts and assuming that they are "a bad person." Or they believe their parents (or friends' parents) have looked at certain external trappings—hair styles, clothing, music—and assumed bad things about their hearts and motives.

 Quite a few kids are convinced their parents are judging their hearts and assuming that they are "a bad person."

Remember, almost all kids view themselves as good kids, even if they sometimes do bad things. And they desperately hope that their parents will somehow separate *them* from the *things they do.*

As one kid put it, "So many parents need to realize that a girl who wears inappropriate clothing might not be a 'filthy ho.' She might just be crying out for love and acceptance... Just give her that!"

"If I Ever Get in Trouble, You'd Better Believe I'm Going to My Dad."

As we figure out how to respond to our children's need for security—especially during their mistakes—it may help to ask ourselves, *What's the worst thing that could happen if I threw my arms around this little hellion right now? What bad thing would he take away from that?* In telling the parable of the prodigal son, Jesus wanted his listeners to know that God—as the father—is loving and forgiving and that he pursues each one of us. Will we not do the same for our own children?

One teenage girl's comment perfectly sums up what happens when our kids know they are secure in our love—and how simply we can communicate our unconditional support:

> One day my dad and I were swimming together. He said one sentence that I'll never forget. "I'd prefer you didn't get in trouble, but if you ever do, I'm here for you." That's all he had to say. Just once. If I ever do get in trouble, you'd better believe I'm going to my dad.

Security

Six

CAN YOU HEAR ME NOW?

Why your teen is convinced he can't talk to you, and how to change his mind

Kids tend to stop talking because they perceive parents as rotten listeners but will open up when we prove we're safe and calmly acknowledge their feelings before addressing a problem.

Picture this scenario: Your daughter stomps in the door after school, steaming mad about being excluded from something and being embarrassed in front of her friends. She doesn't share her innermost thoughts much anymore, so you're glad to have a chance to listen as she vents for a while. When you're finally able to get a word in edgewise, you say, "Well, would it help to do such-and-such?"

She glares at you, mutters, "You never listen to me," then stalks off to text message a friend. You're left speechless, wondering what she thought you were doing for the last fifteen minutes!

"You Just Don't Listen to Me!"

In our interviews, the kids' number one most common complaint about their parents was, "They don't listen." We tried to stifle our snorts at the irony, since that's usually our line about *them*!

In fact, most of us parents deeply wish our kids wouldn't be quite so stingy about sharing what's going on. Not to mention that when we *do* manage to get a conversation going, it all too often degenerates into accusations of, "You just don't understand!" or, "You aren't listening!"

In the face of what we perceive as utter irrationality, it's all too easy to get so irritated by the communication impasse that we shut down any extra effort at listening. Why knock ourselves out if our efforts are so unwanted and if we can't win anyway?

The good news—no, the stupendous news—is that our kids actually *want* to talk to us. The bad news is that the reason they don't—the reason they so often clam up or get irritated with us—is that in their experience we are simply rotten listeners.

 The good news—no, the stupendous news—is that our kids actually *want* to talk to us.

Look how two very representative kids put it:

- "My parents do not listen, and then I just bottle the emotions. But if you'll listen, your kids *will* open up."
- "My dad doesn't understand how emotional I get, and he doesn't know how to deal with my junk."

These two quotes encapsulate the whole point of this chapter: our kids want a listening ear, but we need to know how to listen in the way they need. And the "how," ironically enough, starts with actively focusing on all those swirling emotions that most of us try to avoid!

Let's look at this in more detail.

A Teen Translation Guide to Listening

Let's just accept that the kids are telling the truth when they say that they *want* to talk with us but that they censor themselves—or give up in frustration—because they're convinced we're no good at this listening thing. But what do they really mean by that?

"You don't listen to me" = "You aren't hearing what I feel."

It turns out that, for our kids, listening means hearing and acknowledging what they are *feeling* about a problem, first and foremost. Believe it or not, this is the same thing Jeff and I (Shaunti) told men about their wives in *For Men Only* after our research demonstrated

Listening

that most women need to have their feelings heard before they will be interested in working on a solution. So we were a bit surprised when our teenage research demonstrated that both girls *and* boys need feelings heard first.

We're not sure exactly when boys grow into men who don't care as much about having their feelings heard and who say (in nice deep voices), "Just tell me how to fix it." But at least through age seventeen (the last year we surveyed about this), they still need the same feelings-oriented response as girls.

Look at the fascinating responses to our survey question about how parents should handle a common scenario:

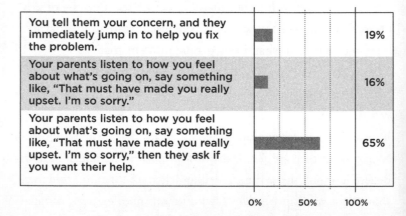

Imagine that you're having a problem with an unfair teacher. If you tell your parents about it, which would be the best way for them to handle it? Choose one answer.

You tell them your concern, and they immediately jump in to help you fix the problem.	19%
Your parents listen to how you feel about what's going on, say something like, "That must have made you really upset. I'm so sorry."	16%
Your parents listen to how you feel about what's going on, say something like, "That must have made you really upset. I'm so sorry," then they ask if you want their help.	65%

0%   50%   100%

Eight out of ten kids—both boys and girls—said that instead of wanting parents to jump in to fix a problem, they first needed parents to hear, acknowledge, and tend to the emotions behind the problem. And only then, most kids said, should parents ask if they want help.

"You don't listen to me" = "Your feelings are getting in the way of hearing mine."

Perhaps one reason it's so imperative to listen to the feelings first is the emotional state teenagers bring to the table. Family therapist Dr. Julie Carbery tells parents that no, their child isn't unusual or putting it on; it really is *normal* for teenagers to be "giant, quivering balls of emotion." And the kids told us those intense emotions can actually feel pretty scary—and prevent them from feeling in control or able to listen in a rational manner. And when they're swept up by emotion, they're on high alert for signals that you are too.

As these quotes illustrate, our kids assume that we can't possibly be listening when we're caught up in our own jangling emotions:

- "My dad yelled at me for an hour because I didn't answer my phone. I was grounded, no questions asked, no explanations heard."

- "My dad will hear only part of what I tell him. He'll hear me yelling, jump to conclusions, and start taking it out on me. He doesn't even know the whole story, and he's freaking out. He won't let me explain, even though I want to and need to, and not letting me will just make things worse."

Listening

Again, kids aren't always rational about this. The last teen quoted wanted his dad to be calm even when he wasn't, and sees no inconsistency in that.

"You don't listen to me" = "You appear to make up your mind before hearing me out."

Among the endless examples the kids gave us, the most common indication of parents not listening was that they seemed to have made up their minds about something in advance—especially the need to implement discipline—and weren't willing to hear explanations. This, in turn, implied that Mom and Dad didn't care. Look at these representative comments:

- "My parents will not listen to me. They say, 'You did this, and we know it. Just shut up and go to your room!' There's never any room for my side of the story, and if I told it, they wouldn't understand or change their minds."

- "They give us the hardest consequences when they haven't even heard the whole story. But that makes us want to rebel. They need to talk to us instead of grounding us from everything before they've heard our side...actually listen to us."

"You don't listen to me" = "You're more concerned with making your point than considering mine."

Have you ever found yourself slipping into lecture mode when you try to help your child see where he went wrong? Kids say that instead of getting through to them, these one-sided talks just confirm their suspicions that parents want a soapbox moment and aren't interested in anything their kid has to say.

- "When my dad says, 'I'd like to give you a little lecture about why you shouldn't do this,' I just about die. I know it's not going to be short, and he's going to lose me after about two minutes."
- "Parents don't understand that kids don't need a big, philosophical answer. Or a big story. Just a short, to-the-point answer or explanation after they've heard you. Otherwise, it's like what Charlie Brown and Lucy and Linus all heard when adults spoke: 'Woh wa wa-wa-wa.' "

"You don't listen to me" = "You seem to care more about enforcing the rules than about our relationship."

At the other extreme, many kids (rightly or wrongly) believe that inflexibility, ultrastrictness, or an unwillingness to explain their reasoning for punishments means that parents care more about the rules than about the relationship with their child.

As one put it, "When we are punished, so many of us feel like our parents won't take the time to let us talk about it and explain our circumstances, or to fully explain the reasoning behind the punishment. Kids want parents to really discuss things and look at life from a 'relationship over rules' perspective."

"You don't listen to me" = "I don't feel safe talking to you."

Teens feel compelled to share the details of life with someone. Even those monosyllabic boys *do* feel a need to talk. It's just a question of whom they're willing to talk *to*. Most said they'd like that to be their parents—at least some of the time.

But one teen explained how difficult it can be to take that risk: "We do want to tell our parents things because if you're open and honest with your parents, they won't punish you. But if you don't tell them things and then they find out, you're sunk! It's just the talking and trusting that's hard."

"No freaking out." (In other words, no strong emotion.)

As we listened to the kids discuss the challenges of talking with their parents, we realized that they're a lot like skittish little deer, warily eying us for our reaction. And the slightest *over*reaction on our part sends them scrambling away…and makes them more cautious about approaching us the next time.

 The slightest *over*reaction on our part sends kids scrambling away…and makes them more cautious about approaching us the next time.

Confirming our observation, three out of four kids on the survey said they'd like to share things with their parents, if they could be reassured that their parents wouldn't flip:

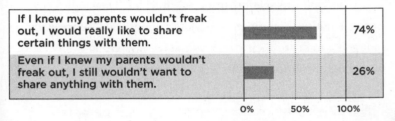

Many teens say there are certain things that they might want to share with their parents but don't because they don't want them to freak out. Which of the following sentences best describes you? Choose one answer.

If I knew my parents wouldn't freak out, I would really like to share certain things with them.	74%
Even if I knew my parents wouldn't freak out, I still wouldn't want to share anything with them.	26%

0%   50%   100%

As one teen said, "I'd love to talk with my parents more. I need them, but I am afraid that they'll overreact if they really know what's going on in my heart and life."

"And don't flip out over good news either."

Would you believe that strongly expressed *positive* comments are also considered freaking out? Apparently positive "overreaction" makes our skittish little deer uncomfortable too.

I (Lisa) finally realized this when one of my daughters said of a guy we both knew, "I know I'm not allowed to date yet, but when I *am,* this is the guy I'd like to go out with."

Listening

"Oh, that's great!" I responded. "I love that kid!"

Instantly, she said, "Oh, I knew you'd freak out if I told you this."

Huh? I said to myself. But on another survey question, well over half of the kids agreed that they would indeed have viewed that scenario as freaking out. And our interviews confirmed that displaying any strong emotion is a real parent no-no in the kid world. Only *they* are allowed to be histrionic, remember?

One kid's explanation made us chuckle: "Freaking out is any strong emotion. You can even freak out about good things. Kids are not going to say to their parents, 'You are now being overly expressive about this situation.' We'll say, 'Stop freaking out.'"

 "Kids are not going to say to their parents, 'You are now being overly expressive about this situation.' We'll say, 'Stop freaking out.'"

Another kid advised, "Parents, be calmer! I didn't tell my mom until two weeks ago that I got my first kiss last year. I casually said one day, 'Yeah, kissing's okay.' She said, 'What? You've kissed? Why didn't you tell me?' Uh, because you'd flip, that's why."

When trust isn't there.

Not surprisingly, a kid who feels his parents aren't listening or can't be trusted with his "stuff" is less likely to risk sharing a problem the next time around. And when kids stop communicating with parents, it can have some pretty heart-wrenching results—because our kids will find *someone* to listen and share with them.

Look at the story one teenager told us:

> My friend couldn't talk to her parents, so she went to an
> aunt to talk about the sexual temptation she was facing.
> The aunt didn't have the same values as the parents,
> though, and she gave her niece birth-control pills! My
> friend said it was the most compassionate thing anyone
> had ever done for her. But I just kept thinking how *sad*
> that she couldn't talk to her own mom…that she didn't
> have that kind of relationship where she could get both
> understanding *and* a better solution that was more in line
> with the family's morals.

What Says, "I'm Listening," to Your Child?

With all the challenges and temptations our kids face, it's important that they *believe* we are safe and clued-in listeners who can be trusted to handle anything they tell us.

Thankfully, the kids provided lots of great examples of what makes them feel we *are* listening, beginning with the revelation that we mentioned earlier.

Listening

1. Focusing on their feelings first.

We should note that although this is probably the most important signal of listening, it was also the most difficult for the kids to articulate. But since the *For Men Only* research had shown us what to look for, we quickly realized we were hearing the "needing feelings heard" comments *everywhere*.

Don't filter out the emotion; focus on it.

Because teenagers so often express their emotions in excessive or hurtful ways, parents may be inclined to filter out the feelings and focus on the problem at hand in order to figure out how to help this kid who is so upset. Yet, the national survey indicated that it's far more productive to do the opposite: filter out the *problem* for a minute in order to figure out what your child is feeling, and acknowledge it.

As we saw in the survey question on page 116, the vast majority of kids indicated they want parents to address their emotions before they jump to the fix. And on a similar survey question, the older the kids got, the more they said that acknowledging their feelings best proves a parent is listening. Then they may or may not *need* our help with the problem itself. Consider these comments:

- "I just need to be heard out. Then it's fine."
- "It's just important to talk and not keep things inside. That's a huge part of the fix."

- "Sometimes listening can fix the problem."
- "When you say it to someone, you hear it differently, and often it all works out."

Where possible, **affirm** *the feelings.*

Focusing on our child's emotions about a problem, then, is the starting point of good listening. But what completes the teens' sense of being heard is our empathy with those feelings. In addition, teens really appreciate hearing that they're not "weird" for feeling as they do. It makes a big difference when parents not only help their children talk through their feelings but also acknowledge and affirm those feelings as legitimate.

After a big fight between her boys, one wise mom helped her son feel heard by saying, "Scott, I see that privacy is really important to you. Do you wish all your stuff was locked in your room with a big deadbolt, so that no one could touch it? Yeah… I wish I could protect some things from being messed with, too."

2. Providing an oasis of calm in the midst of their emotional storms.

It may seem unfair, but in order to be convinced that we're listening, teens need us to remain calm even when they aren't. After talking to countless kids in focus groups and shopping malls, we realized that their intensity doesn't just come from hyperemotionalism but from some *serious* tension. When dealing with a concern or conflict, the typical teenager becomes like a tightly coiled, knotted rubber band, and she has to be loosened up before she can talk and think rationally.

We can help our kids loosen up by letting them spout out all those jangling feelings and then by affirming those feelings. But as they unravel and process their emotions, they need us to keep our own feelings under control.

They need to see that you are remaining as calm as possible.

Hard as it is for us to pull off at times, our kids say it helps them believe that we really are listening when we project an air of peace. Obviously, we can't always be completely calm, and sometimes our children will see us getting upset. But just the fact that we're trying speaks volumes about our willingness to listen, as this comments reveals:

> When I told my dad I had tried weed, he said, "Well,
> that was a stupid move," whereas Mom just flipped out.
> Both of them told me it was wrong, but in totally differ-
> ent ways. I can talk to Dad.

And look at the mutual trust built by one single mom who demonstrated, even while being firm in consequences, that she was listening to her son and prioritizing their relationship. Her high-school age son told us, "I can tell my mom anything. I know that even when she's ticked at me and going to ground me, she's willing to listen to what happened and what I think about it."

What a difference it makes when we strive for calmness, even if our insides are trembling in the face of their attitude or revelations—and even when their body language triggers our impulse to fight.

Help them recognize their own body language.

Believe it or not, the childhood development experts confirm that kids actually don't realize when they're sending us "fight mode" signals. Consider this extremely helpful advice from Dr. Carbery, who sees this every day in her family practice:

> Since kids don't know how they're coming across, it actually helps a lot if parents will say, "You know, Son, you have your arms crossed and you are pacing and you are talking in a much louder voice than usual." Often the kid will go, "Really?" And when they uncross their arms, sit down in a chair, and talk in a normal voice, suddenly, the situation becomes more workable.

Try not to take hurtful things to heart.

Although we want to teach our kids to recognize their hurtful words and actions and to practice self-control and respect, we also need to keep in mind this advice from the kids themselves: try not to get so

upset about what they say when *they* are upset. One kid advised:
"Just so you know, if a teen says, 'I hate you,' don't take it to heart.
He'll love you again the next day."

3. Proving that we're "safe" listeners.

As we've seen, our kids need to feel generally secure with us in order
to talk with us about the things that matter to them. That sense of
security also is necessary for them to believe that we'll be willing to
listen even if we disagree with their viewpoint.

So in addition to remaining calm, being understanding, and
providing the other elements of security described in the previous
chapter, here are a few things the kids say we can do to help them
feel safe enough to open up.

Err on the side of a willingness to believe them, even if you don't agree with them.

The kids seemed to be deeply reassured that we're listening if we signal our willingness to trust what they tell us, even when there's a
problem. As one advised:

> If my folks are interrupting me and cutting me off all
> the time, I know they don't believe what I'm saying. But
> if they say, "I understand," and ask follow-up questions,
> I know that they aren't just sitting there, nodding their
> heads but ignoring everything I say.

And as one teen explained, trusting them seems to create a two-way street:

> When your parents trust you, things will go better. And if there really *is* a problem I know I can trust *them* enough to say, "Hey, I made a bad decision last night. Can we talk about it?"

Probe below the surface.

The kids say their parents are too often content with surface answers and thereby miss the great opportunities for connection that would come if they pressed in just a little bit more.

- "There are so many things we need to tell our parents, but they're so busy that we don't want to bother them. But if they would take the time and push into our lives a little more, even when we look like we're backing away, it would help a lot."

Kids say their parents are too often content with surface answers and thereby miss great opportunities for connection.

- "Parents usually take things at face value and don't press in to really hear what's deeper on a kid's mind. Sometimes we just need them to ask a few more questions, take a little more time, and it'll all spill out like Niagara Falls."

Listening

We also got this advice on how to press in:

> A question like "How was your day?" can be a bad probe because it is expected and surface-y. But "How is every-thing *else* in your life?" is a good probe because it's an open question that digs below the surface. So we know that our parents have a genuine concern about our well-being, but without the abrasive or threatening questions like why we were out late. If they would give us a good probe from the start, it would give us the opportunity to vent and come clean about some things that were proba-bly on our parents' agenda to ask us anyway.

Treat their "stuff" with care.

The kids were unanimous on this: if we want our kids to even con-sider talking openly about things, parents must take seriously teenage concerns about privacy and how something might "look," even if we can't see why it's a big deal. As one cautioned: "I can't talk about who I like with my parents. I feel like it'll backfire on me. They could slip up and say something over the top in front of my friends, just joking around. I love their sense of humor, but they have to be more careful or they won't get told as much."

Thankfully, we were encouraged to hear of many parents who were being careful with the things that mattered to their kids. As one teen girl put it, "I'm comfortable telling my parents things because they've proven that when I ask them to keep the conversation private, they will."

The Reward: Connection with Your Kid

In the rush of everyday life, nothing demonstrates our love and care to our kids quite like our sincere listening. And in the uncertainty, confusion, and excitement of their growing years, nothing seems to cement a parent-child relationship more than the child's belief that he will be heard.

We leave you with this compelling example, provided by a recently married twenty-two-year-old man, of how a parent's calm listening skills and wisdom made a huge difference during his teenage years:

When I was in middle and high school, one of the coolest things was that I could always talk to my dad about things I was dealing with. Porn, maturing, whatever… He never acted shocked.

In tenth grade, for example, I was really worried that I might be gay. I was recognizing good-looking guys and envying them. Looking back, I now know that guys that age haven't completely learned how to identify with the same and opposite sex in a healthy mind-set, but at the time I was freaked out that I thought another guy was good-looking. I knew if I could talk to anyone about this, it would be my dad. He helped me see that I was a normal, developing guy and that my feelings were actually just envy. He literally said, "Don't worry, Son. You're not gay. You just want to be good-looking like them, and you will be. You are already."

Suddenly I wasn't anxious anymore. I'm so thankful I could talk to my dad, and he could listen and give me the perspective I needed.

What that father did required no PhD, and it wasn't rocket science; he simply listened to what was going on in his son's heart, acknowledged it, and reassured him. And he had built up enough trust that his son was willing to risk going to him in the first place.

Regardless of the current state of your relationship with the jangling bundle of emotions that lives in *your* house, it's never too late for you to do the same.

Seven

ATTITUDE ADJUSTMENT

What mood swings reveal about teens' secret fears, and how you can boost their confidence

What looks like an attitude problem may actually be a sign of insecurity, but actively countering our children's fears can build their confidence and help them become more respectful of parents and others.

It's enough to drive even the most reasonable parent right over the edge.

You ask your son to take out the trash, but instead of moving to respond he stays seated, intently focused on rearranging the crumbs on his plate. After your second, slightly more testy request, he mutters, "Fine," shoves back his chair, and shoulders a bag of trash out to the garage, where you hear him slamming the lids on the garbage cans. When he comes back in, you pause in your dishwashing to ask, "Is anything wrong?"

He shakes his head. When you press him, he gives you a sullen glare and retorts, "I said nothing's wrong. Give it a rest." He stalks off, and soon electronic blasting noises from the basement suggest some video game aliens are bearing the brunt of his unexplained wrath.

Or, you're trying to show your daughter how to wash her car in a way that won't leave streaks. Suddenly she grabs the sponge and snaps, "Okay, I get it. I get it!" Shocked, you open your mouth to respond, but your daughter interrupts again. "I know, I know. *I'm being disrespectful.* I'll just go to my room to save you the trouble of sending me there."

Either of those scenarios sound familiar?

Underneath the Attitude

For most parents, nothing raises our hackles so quickly as for our kids to cop an attitude with us. When we see those rolled eyeballs, a hoity-toity posture, or sullen discontent, a head of steam builds up in our brains, and we get the urge to knock that attitude down a peg or two.

Now, we're trying to help our kids grow into the mature, respectful, self-confident individuals God intends them to be, and that certainly involves helping them learn to control their words and behavior. But in our research we were surprised to discover that those infuriating teenage attitudes are often just the outward sign of underlying, secret fears and insecurities—insecurities that stand between our children and the confident adults they long to become.

Through our focus groups and kid-on-the-street interviews, we gathered some key insights in this area that could—over time—change the dynamics between many frustrated parents and children. Armed with this knowledge, we can not only avoid triggering those secret fears and insecurities, but we can also actively counteract them by building up our kids' self-confidence.

Of course, no matter how wisely and lovingly we communicate with them, our children have to make their own choices about how to communicate with us. But by applying these findings, we'll make it easier for them to choose the path of respect more often.

Gender matters.

Almost every time I (Shaunti) speak to a group about my *For Women Only* findings, I get this query during question-and-answer time: "Well, if you say men most need respect and secretly fear being inadequate, what does that mean for my son?"

This whole book was initially birthed out of a desire to find the answer to that question. Although most factors behind the behavior that baffles parents ended up being universal and not gender-driven, there were a few critical and undeniable differences in what each gender needs and in the corresponding secret insecurities that erupt into bad attitudes.

Attitude

How we came to these conclusions.

We should note that we found ourselves treading carefully as we dug into this subject. The girls, especially, often bristled with the modern female's skepticism at the suggestion that boys and girls might have different needs. Yet when we set aside all philosophical discussions and simply asked questions, the patterns emerged unmistakably and at once.

Putting girls and boys in separate focus groups, we started with a blank whiteboard in each room and wrote down the kids' answers to our questions about what they most fear and what most builds their confidence. Neither group knew what the other had said until their own chart of responses was completed. At that point, even the most vocal gender-difference doubters were silenced by the obvious, powerful differences between the two sexes.

In the gender-specific sections to follow, you'll find simplified charts showing those results, which we then tested in a follow-up survey.*

In the end, seven out of ten *boys* most wanted to feel respected, believed in, and encouraged in their individual impact; and six out of ten most feared failure, being inadequate or disrespected, and appearing weak or powerless.

Conversely, seven out of ten *girls* most needed to feel loved,

---

* For the survey, we removed or altered the words that would signal an obvious gender direction (such as changing the oft-stated female need to feel "lovely" to the gender-neutral "attractive"). The full results can be found at our website.

accepted, and special; and three out of four most feared rejection, and not being lovely or unique in the eyes of others.

We're not psychologists or sociologists, but in the most general sense, these results suggest this:

- Guys most want to be recognized for what they do, and they most fear failure. And...
- Girls most want to be valued for who they are, and they most fear rejection.**

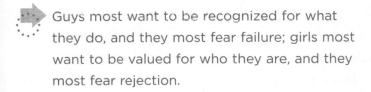

Guys most want to be recognized for what they do, and they most fear failure; girls most want to be valued for who they are, and they most fear rejection.

So let's look separately at what these revelations mean when it comes to the external attitudes of boys and girls—and the different ways we can help them overcome the insecurities that hold them back.

Attitude

** Obviously, we are by necessity simplifying complex issues and making significant generalizations to which there will be exceptions. Also, when we say something like, "Boys need respect," we are in no way suggesting that girls don't! We're simply reporting the undeniable patterns we've seen in our research about what was *most* important to each group.

A Man in the Making

Not long ago, I (Lisa) got a hands-on lesson in how to help a son deal with his insecurities…and how not to. My then-eleven-year-old, Brandon, came into the house, red-faced and angry. When I pressed him, he said a bunch of guys on the brand-new neighborhood raft in the lake were slinging mud into his face and his buddy's, which was both causing pain and ruining the raft. When I charged down to the lake to give the older boys a lecture, I noticed Brandon's friend shaking his head in disgust. He later called Brandon a wuss—or worse—because Mom had to come and fix things for her baby. So then Brandon got sullen with *me*.

That evening, my wise husband, Eric, counseled me that boys need to start fighting their own battles at age eleven or twelve. He said that Brandon just needed his feelings of frustration, shame, and powerlessness acknowledged (there's that listening principle again!) and then needed a few tools to fight his own battles. I apologized to Brandon for interfering and making things worse, and Eric took the opportunity to teach him a few simple wrestling moves.

The next day, the name-calling "friend" tried it again in front of the other kids. Brandon swiftly pinned him to the ground and held him there until he apologized. Word swept through the neighborhood that Brandon wasn't someone to be messed with. When Eric heard the details, he said, "Son, I'm glad you did that, and I don't think he'll mess with you again. I bet you'll be buddies again in a few days. I'm proud of you for knowing how to defend yourself. Some day you may have to defend others too."

Eric's positive, empowering response tapped into what every parent needs to know about helping a boy conquer his fears and feed his confidence.

What most gives him confidence—and what undermines it.

The chart below reflects a simplified version of what we heard in the focus groups when we asked the boys what they most feared—and what most gives them confidence to overcome those fears:

"I most fear..."	"I most need to feel..."
• failure	• able
• feeling inadequate	• successful
• being watched and found wanting	• that people are watching and commenting on my success
• feeling powerless	• respected
• appearing weak	• accomplished
• not being respected	• powerful
• not being the best at something	• that I'm looked up to
• no one noticing when I achieve something	• significant

Attitude

Comments explaining those needs and insecurities *poured* out of the guys in our focus groups. Here's a representative sampling:

- "If you feel trusted, you will succeed. That's a guy's thought process. But if people don't think you're adequate, then you're *not* trusted, not respected, and that's the worst feeling of all. We want to be in control, to feel like we can handle things without anyone else's help."

- "If I feel I can't get there, I usually won't even try, so I don't risk the humiliation. The feeling you'll not be able to get there is *debilitating* to a guy."

- "I'd rather feel dominant, and if people don't like me, it's okay with me. I want to be powerful. I want to conquer. Every guy has his list of superpowers."

- "In the movie *Batman Begins,* Bruce Wayne tells his girlfriend something like, 'It's not who you are; it's what you do.' That is such an adequacy quote, and that's how we feel as guys. We're always being judged by what we're doing or not doing—*not who we are inside*" (emphasis ours).

They need to feel respected, regardless of whether they've earned it.

As we've seen, a guy's greatest fear is being a failure or, more specifically, being *perceived* as a failure. Close on its heels are the evil cousins of feeling inadequate and disrespected. And to overcome that insidious self-doubt, every male, old or young, deeply needs to know that those closest to him respect him as a person, regardless of his inevitable mistakes.

As noted in *For Women Only,* Emerson Eggerichs, author of the excellent book *Love and Respect,* nails this critical point about understanding any male: "We've become such a love-dominated culture... so we've come to think that love should be unconditional, but respect must be earned. Instead, what men need is *unconditional respect*—to be respected for who they are, apart from how they do."

 Every male, old or young, deeply needs to know that those closest to him respect him as a person, regardless of his inevitable mistakes.

In other words what most gives a teen boy confidence is not just accomplishment, dominance, and success; what's even *more* important is, as one guy put it, "The internal feeling that you can *get* to success...and then other people watching and commenting on your success, and respecting you for it. *That* is powerful."

He often perceives disrespect, even where none is intended.

Like their dads, most boys are ultrasensitive to signs that they are *not* believed in, *not* respected, *not* dominant or powerful. And based on the examples the guys gave us, we believe that many parents have no idea they're sending those signals. For example, one boy told us,

"Recently I was sure I got a job at a game store, but my mom said, 'You can't be too confident, you know. Keep applying elsewhere, just to be safe.' It made me mad that she didn't believe in me."

 Most boys are ultrasensitive to signs that they are *not* believed in, and many parents have no idea they're sending those signals.

We highly doubt that his mom didn't believe in him, but that's the message he heard. Her simple comment was probably intended to protect and help her son. But he didn't want to be protected; he wanted to fly—and to have his mom believe that he could. And if his maiden flight ended in a crash landing, well, *then* he could use a little comforting...and encouragement to get right back in the game.

The signal that he's feeling insecure: sullenness or anger.

Since teenage boys aren't the most talkative bunch on the planet, how can you spot when your son is feeling inadequate, powerless, disrespected, or like a failure—whether due to something you've said or some other circumstance in his world? Well, this is often where "attitude" raises its ugly head. A boy who is feeling disrespected will likely become angry, sullen, or withdrawn.

The results from our national survey confirmed what many parents have observed.

If something happens to make you feel powerless and disrespected, how are you likely to react? Choose all correct answers.

Percentage of guys who chose one or more of the following:		99.5%
I would be angry.		67%
I would get quiet and think it over.		51%
I would be sullen and grumpy.		34%
I'd stuff it and probably blow up later.		30%
I would compensate by trying to be powerful and respected in another area.		21%
I would blow up.		15%
Percentage of guys who chose one or more of the following:		24%
I would pour out all my feelings to a friend.		18%
I'd cry.		12%

Note: Because respondents could choose more than one answer, percentages don't add up to 100%.

0%   50%   100%

As you can see, the two answers guys chose most often were *anger* and *quietness*. Nearly 100 percent of our male survey-takers said if they were feeling powerless or disrespected they would get angry, quiet, grumpy, stuff the problem, or compensate in another area. Very few said they would share their feelings with someone else—which is, we suspect, the *most* likely response for girls!

Look at these characteristic guy comments about their typical response to feeling powerless or disrespected:

- "Yeah, that happened at school this week. I was so angry that I was literally clenching my fists under the desk."
- "I just retreat into my room and throw things."
- "If I'm ticked off, I'll just get quiet—for a very long time."

How to Build Him Up

So what do we do if we see withdrawal and a closed-off spirit, and suspect that our son is feeling powerless or disrespected? First, we may need to look at whether *we* could be unintentionally triggering those insecurities and work through the specific applications for those things that we can control and change. But since many factors beyond our control also impact a boy's sense of confidence, here are a few essential ways to help him overcome his insecurities as he moves toward the future.

1. Respect him, regardless.

First and foremost, we need to demonstrate respect to our sons whether or not we think they've earned it. If this concept seems foreign, you might consider how you would respond to a daughter's need for unconditional love. We would never say, "How am I supposed to love you when you've lied to me?" Yet it's just as devastating for a boy to hear that we can't respect him until he earns it.

 We need to demonstrate respect to our sons whether or not we think they've earned it.

Yes, your son will make mistakes—and that's precisely when he most needs your encouragement and an *unconditional* demonstration of your respect for him as a person. By honoring and supporting your son *through* his mistakes, even as you apply any necessary consequences, you'll help him feel like—and then become—the *respect*able man he longs to be.

2. Use the language of honor.

Most of us—especially women—are good at demonstrating love, but often we don't even know when we're showing disrespect or doubt. Even our body language or tone of voice can make a guy feel utterly shredded.

Wherever you are right now, humor us: Put down this book for moment, stand up, cross your arms over your chest, put your weight on your back leg, stare at a point about five feet away, and raise your eyebrows in disbelief. You are now giving what the teen boys described to us as "the death stare"—a look that conveys utter contempt and condescension.

Dr. Eggerichs told us in an interview, "Those are lethal gestures....

A teen boy's spirit will deflate, and so will all fond feelings. He'll clench his fist, grind his teeth, and do what you tell him…but he won't be affectionate."

One teen guy confirmed that perspective: "My mom makes me feel like a five-year-old who ought to be ashamed of himself. I can't wait to graduate and get out of there."

Learning to catch that body language and use the verbal language of honor instead will help us replace those unintentionally demeaning messages with confidence-building encouragement. Dr. Eggerichs suggests that we stop focusing solely on saying, "I love you," and begin saying things like, "You know what I really respect about you, Todd? You're becoming a man of honor. I'm really proud that you didn't let your sister provoke you."

Carefully study this quote about a dad who caught his responsible, athletic son taking drugs:

When my dad found out that I smoked pot, he said,
"You may not understand the danger, Son, but weed is
so much stronger than it used to be. Athletes like you
can't handle that stuff. It's not wise." That's all I needed
to hear. Never touched the stuff again.

Look at it: "Athletes like you…" Instantly, the kid feels ten feet tall! His dad thinks he's a strong, powerful athlete, and he wants to live up to that.

Using the language of honor may not come naturally, but seeing its impact on our sons will give us the incentive to make it a habit.

3. Recognize both effort and success.

As we saw in our interviews, the greatest motivator for guys isn't just success; rather, it is having someone they respect *notice* that success. Giving regular affirmation, encouragement, and praise is one of the most effective ways to build confidence in our sons and create a positive cycle. As one guy put it, "Recognition and praise fuel success."

Giving regular affirmation, encouragement, and praise is one of the most effective ways to build confidence in our sons and create a positive cycle.

One simple statement that encapsulates our respect and affirmation is, "I'm proud of you." Look at this teenage boy's comment: "This year I got a job, and Dad said, 'I'm so proud of you. You have accomplished something so great all on your own.' That was huge. He was affirming my adulthood."

4. Value Dad's unique role.

It's essential to let fathers approach parenting in the ways that they are uniquely designed for. And that usually means we moms have to back off! When this subject comes up in my (Shaunti's) talks to women, frequently someone will protest, "But my husband is not a good dad. He's withdrawn…left the playing field…absent." And yet as we talk, the woman quite often realizes that he may have checked out because she actually prevented him from being the dad he was designed to be by wanting him to do things her way.

A father's affirmation in particular carries huge significance for boys. Look at one representative comment:

> I really messed up at a tae kwon do tournament. I was
> quiet on the ride home, and after a while, Dad told me
> how he felt when he lost a big baseball game in high
> school. When a father does that, you know you're not
> alone. He's affirming that it's okay, and still masculine
> to feel that way. That's a big deal for a guy.

Boys need fathers or, at the very least, good male role models. If you're a single mom and your son's dad isn't in the picture, you'll want to look for ways to connect your boy with a positive male influence.

5. Give your son opportunities to rise to the occasion.

Similarly, at some point we have to stop hovering and let our boys attempt things on their own.

After one speaking engagement where I (Shaunti) talked about how trust and respect empower men, a woman said she had finally realized how to handle a problem with her sixteen-year-old son. He mowed her friends' lawns for money, and some of them had been calling her to complain that he hadn't trimmed this or cut that properly. After her repeated and unsuccessful attempts to get him to "do things right," the clients were upset, she was embarrassed, he was feeling pressured, and their relationship was going downhill.

Taking to heart her new insights on men, she went home and told her son that this was his business and she was trusting him to handle it on his own, sink or swim. She told her friends, "Here's his cell phone number. Call him directly, and if he doesn't respond to your satisfaction, then fire him and hire someone else." She told her son that she believed he could rise to the occasion of doing things without her.

Months later, I followed up with her. Although there were still a few ups and downs, she said her new strategy had "made things so much better." Her son, thankful that she was willing to step back, told her that since he was acting responsibly in other areas of his life, he knew he could be responsible with this as well. Best of all, her demonstration of respect had greatly improved their relationship.

In a similar way, when it comes to discipline and rules, some boys may need us to draw bigger boundaries than we might be comfortable with, allowing them room to make mistakes and prove to us and themselves that they can do better the next time.

You know best what your child will respond to, but you may find it interesting that six out of ten guys on our follow-up survey said that if their parents would be willing to let them make mistakes and try again instead of immediately restricting the boundaries, they wouldn't "play the system" but would be honorable.

The Confident Man Inside

As part of their very fabric, boys *want* to "wow" us with their abilities and are motivated to rise to the occasion when we raise the bar of expectation along a soundtrack of praise. And based on all our research, we're confident that as you consistently express respect for your son's efforts, those sullen, angry, insecurity-fed attitudes gradually will be cast aside by a confident young man who is ready to fly.

The Emerging Woman of Worth

Think about the stories that so often capture the imaginations of little girls…stories like "Cinderella," "Snow White," and "The Ugly Duckling." One recent "ugly duckling" movie, *The Princess Diaries,* initially shows a teen girl (played by Anne Hathaway) living out the worst fear of most young girls: feeling ordinary, unloved, invisible. She doesn't fit in, and she's being giggled about and rejected by those around her. And then she finds out that she's not ordinary; she's a princess. It takes time, but she eventually learns how to stand tall and have confidence in herself.

As little girls, our daughters beam when they don the beautiful ball-gown costumes of a Disney princess because it makes them *feel* like a princess: special and lovely. Ten years later the awkward, developing, lippy versions of those little girls still need to feel lovely and special—inside and out. And perhaps more than ever, they need our help to conquer some deep-seated fears and grow into confident, engaging young women.

What most gives her confidence—and what sabotages it.

While a boy gains confidence by being recognized for his external impact and accomplishments, a girl's confidence comes from being loved and accepted because she is special on the inside. That's why "being liked" is vitally important to a girl; it assuages her secret fear that others will feel that there's nothing worthy in her and reject her. Look at what triggers a girl's insecurities and what builds confidence:

"I most fear / am most insecure about..."	"I most need to feel..."
• rejection • what people think of me • how I look • being talked about behind my back • not being included • having people think something negative about me that isn't true • not being known, accepted, and liked • not being unique or valuable • being invisible	• accepted • included • known and liked for who I really am • special • unique • lovely/beautiful inside and out • that others enjoy being around me / are drawn to me • pursued

In our focus groups, the girls were so passionate about discussing these needs and fears that we had a difficult time moving them on to other subjects! Here are just a few representative comments:

A girl's confidence comes from being loved and accepted because she is special on the inside.

- "I want my soul to be revealed. And for people to like and accept me even after they really know me and all of my stuff."
- "I realize that I'm loved, but I never get tired of hearing it."
- "I hate the feeling that I'm hanging out with people who don't really care about *me,* but they just want the security of being with someone—and that they'll probably leave when someone better comes along. It makes me feel used and manipulated…and then I hate myself that I let myself be used and manipulated."

 "I want people to like and accept me even after they really know me and all of my stuff."

- "As a girl, when one of your supposed friends does that 'mean girl' thing and turns on you, it triggers this intense feeling of being disliked and abandoned. They knew me…and rejected me."

Attitude

"Am I worthy of rejection?"

Based on these and similar comments, it's clear that a girl's core fear is not just being rejected but that she is innately "rejectable." Your daughter may be smart, beautiful, even highly popular, but inside she's likely worried that she's simply not special or lovely or lovable enough. Like most girls, she's probably ultrasensitive to negative feedback that implies her fears are justified.

Look at these comments from two beautiful, engaging girls who were in the "popular" crowd at school:

> *Girl 1:* "Secretly, I need to hear, 'You're great, you're awesome, and everyone likes you.' And if you hear that, you feel wanted. But the next day you could go the whole day without anyone talking to you. And that creates this constant depression. You stop trying, and think, *Well, all right, I'll just stand here alone then.*"

> *Girl 2:* "Yeah…a guy may feel the rejection like that once a year when he doesn't make the football team or the girl won't go to homecoming with him. But we feel rejection daily when people don't say hi."

Hair-trigger sensitivity with parents.

Perhaps because they expect Mom and Dad to be secure ports in the storms of their self-confidence, girls may even be *more* sensitive to any signals from parents, however unintentional, that confirm their "rejectability." Look at these comments:

- "My mother used to compare my body shape to my friends'. She'd say, 'Your shoulders are so broad.' Well, what could I possibly do about that? What positive thing could possibly come out of ragging on me about an unchangeable feature? All it did was to confirm that I was unlovable and without power to improve myself."

- "My father used to say to me, 'I need to be alone. I need for you to just disappear for a while.' The man I admired most was asking me to become invisible."

- "Especially at this age, sometimes when a teenager tugs at their parents to get their attention, it's because we are out of options. It's hard when a kid makes the parents a priority and they make the kid an option. I'm like, 'I just want to spend time with my mom today,' and my mom implies she has more important things to do."

The signal that she's feeling insecure: mouthing off.
One of the biggest surprises in all our research was that some of the behaviors parents find most maddening—lippiness, sarcasm, or antagonistic comments—are signals that a girl's deepest insecurities have been triggered. Parents—especially fathers—could easily conclude that the daughter's tirade is rooted in disrespect or a desire to

Attitude

challenge authority. And while those disrespectful feelings may indeed be there, they often mask something much deeper: a profound, internal longing for reassurance. So this is when they need our affirmation most of all; not of the behavior, but of the girl.

Look at the startling results from our survey:

When you're mouthing off to your parents, what feelings are most likely going on inside you? Choose all correct answers.

Percentage of girls who chose one or more of the following:	**98%**
I'm feeling misunderstood.	84%
How I'm reacting to my parents may not have as much to do with them as it does with what is going on in my life right now.	51%
I'm feeling fearful, anxious, or defensive.	50%
I'm just not feeling great about myself right now.	48%
I'm feeling unloved, unappreciated, or neglected.	44%
Percentage of girls who chose one or more of the following:	**56%**
I despise my parents.	42%
I'm trying to attack my parents and make them feel bad.	23%
I know everything, and they know nothing.	19%

Note: Because respondents could choose more than one answer, percentages don't add up to 100%.

0%   50%   100%

Although more than half the girls admitted to feeling pretty nasty when they were mouthing off, nearly all the girls confessed that their sarcastic exterior concealed a host of much more vulnerable feelings. In total, fully *98 percent* of the girls in our survey confessed that their sharp words hid pain over being misunderstood or fearful, or feeling bad about themselves. And half also said that their parents were getting the brunt of emotions that had little to do with them, as the girls worried about other things in their lives and lashed out at those nearest to them.

A cover-up for insecurity.

Look at how some of the girls described the insecurity underneath their back talk:

- "When I'm mouthing off, I'm just saying, 'Quit pretending you understand me!'"
- "When I'm mouthing off, I'm usually feeling misunderstood. No one has ever felt the way I'm feeling... No one understands me or sees exactly how I feel, and I get frustrated."
- "I hope parents realize that there is insecurity under the surface, and if I am feeling fat and ugly and like no one likes me, I may take it out on whoever is nearest—someone who I subconsciously know will love me regardless. And that may be my boyfriend, but it's more likely to be my parents... I know that's not really fair to parents, but I know they won't reject me just because I'm being a jerk."

Attitude

> "If I am feeling fat and ugly and like no one likes me, I may take it out on whoever is nearest."

Even among the girls who admitted to having some pretty nasty feelings while lashing out at their parents, eight out of ten overwhelmingly used a later question to declare how much they loved and appreciated them.

The dark and light sides of the same trait.

This alienating response to feeling insecure affects more people than just her parents. Much of the "mean girl" tendency to make others feel bad about themselves appears to stem from a girl's own insecurities. But we repeatedly heard that this doesn't reflect the person she wants to be. As one representative girl put it:

> You only take your insecurities out on each other when you feel less confident. And if you break that cycle, you're also helping yourself. Making someone feel good about themselves makes us feel good and confident about *ourselves.*

It seems that most girls are designed with a God-given ability to influence how others feel about themselves. But all too often, that predisposition can be hijacked by a girl's insecurities, damaging her relationships and further diminishing her sense of worth.

How to Build Her Up

To help our girls become confident young women who can have a positive impact on others—including us!—we need to both build them up ahead of time so they'll be less vulnerable to demoralizing messages and to reassure them when doubts rear up.

1. Tell her how special she is; don't assume that she knows it.

Because today's school politics can do incredible damage to a girl's sense of inner worth, your daughter desperately needs your affirmation of who she is and who she's becoming. As you might guess, our daughters' longing to feel special runs so deep that if we don't provide the assurance they need, they'll feel compelled to look elsewhere.

Our words carry enormous weight with girls. They store our comments in their memory banks to be brought out later and lingered over. To ensure that plenty of those stored messages are uplifting, we can use starters like, "One thing that's so special about you is…," or, "What I appreciate so much about you is…"

When we asked the girls for examples, we heard dozens. Here are just two:

- "One day, leaving the house, my dad said, 'Bye, pretty girl.' I think about that all the time. *Pretty girl…*"
- "I was telling my mom about all this mean-girl junk that was happening at school, and she surprised me by casually

saying, 'Well, at least you got something productive done. I think it's so great how you can work under pressure.'"

 "One day, leaving the house, my dad said, 'Bye, pretty girl.' I think about that all the time. *Pretty girl...*"

If a girl most needs to feel special, lovely, and loved for who she is, you can imagine how incredibly wounded she'd be by even a *hint* that her parents' belief in her specialness wavers with external factors or her performance in life. Consider this focus group exchange that we're sure would have deeply surprised the mother in question:

> *Girl 1:* "I was so hurt the other day. My mom saw me reaching for a dessert and said, 'Honey, do you really need a cookie?'"
>
> (All the other girls exclaim in shock and sympathy.)
>
> *Girl 2:* "Wow… The only thing worse than being judged by people who *don't* know you is being judged by your parents, who are supposed to know you and love you no matter what."

When pressed, the girls suggested the mother could have expressed her concern positively and without a trace of guilt by saying something like, "You've done so well with eating healthy since school started this fall. I don't want you to be bummed tonight that you didn't meet your goal. How about I make a fruit salad for us instead?" And "never ever *ever*," they said, negatively compare a daughter's looks to another girl by saying something like, "Don't you want to look like so-and-so?"

2. Value Dad's unique role.

Over and over our interviews and our research demonstrated that while daughters need affirmation from both parents, regular encouragement from a father has a particularly powerful, lasting impact. Verbalizing affirmation often comes more naturally to women, but we heard many wonderful examples of fathers who understood the power of positive words:

- "My dad and I go to the mall together. And he says things like, 'Hey, that outfit looks good on that girl, and I bet it would look good on you.' I know he's probably just doing it as an excuse to build me up, but I don't care. I soak that in like a sponge."

 While daughters need affirmation from both parents, regular encouragement from a father has a particularly powerful, lasting impact.

Attitude

- "My dad takes me out on special dates where he really talks and listens to me. It's so fun and encouraging."
- "My dad says he's proud of me, and that I'm pretty. I've always wanted to be a vet, and my dad has always encouraged me in that. He says I can be anything I want."

3. When she's hurting, reassure her—without crowding.

Because teens are torn between their need to pull away and their need for continued affirmation, we heard a lot about parents not crowding their daughters when something made a girl doubt herself. Instead, the girls said, parents should just make it clear they were there, without hovering.

For example, one mom said her touchy daughter responds well to, "I'm sorry you're dreading going to school with those braces. Let's have a frappuccino and forget about it for one blissful moment…" Or even simply, "If you want to vent, I'm here."

It's also worth remembering that sometimes our girls tend to mistrust our assurances, and trying *too* hard to convince them only increases their resistance. As one girl explained:

> If there's something you really, strongly dislike about yourself, if your parents try to build you up, you aren't going to believe it. You won't trust their sincerity. Or, more likely, you start to doubt their judgment. It's

like, *I know my hair looks* terrible; *if Mom keeps insisting it looks nice, she doesn't know what she's talking about.*

In those cases, we may need to say it, back off, and find other ways to affirm our girls. If she won't believe it from Mom, maybe she'll believe it from her older brother.

4. Be aware of the serious manifestations of insecurity—and show you care.

There are many more-serious manifestations of insecurity—such as eating disorders or the widespread trend of teen girls cutting themselves—that go beyond the scope of this book and often require professional counseling. But we wanted to at least show you what two former cutters told us, as encouragement of a parent's power to help alleviate even this angst:

- "I had never been very close to my dad until last year. My mom noticed that I had been cutting and flipped her lid, saying things like, 'Oh my gosh, everything I've been doing as a parent has been wrong!' But my dad came to me and said, 'Listen, I'm not trying to analyze you. I don't want to crowd or judge. But if you *ever* want to talk, I'm here.' With that five-minute conversation, everything changed. The comfort and trust was built with him, and now I go to him all the time."

Attitude

- "When he found out that I'd been cutting, my dad said, 'It makes me sad that you feel you have to do that, that you want to hurt yourself that way.' To me, his words said that he loved me, that he cared about me, that he noticed this, and that it hurt him. I thought, *Wow! Maybe I should talk to him and work it out.* So I did, and I totally stopped cutting."

5. When she's most unlovable, address the disrespect but stay connected.

Unfortunately, when a daughter lashes out, her words can leave us feeling wounded, angry, or alienated. Even if we mentally recognize that she's erupting out of fear or insecurity, our own anger can lead us into a fight-or-flight response, tempting us to either strike back with our own hurtful words or to beat a hasty retreat to protect ourselves from further outbursts. Obviously, neither alternative resolves the inner pain that triggered her attitude problem in the first place.

To make matters worse, many parents—especially fathers—may not recognize when hormones and monthly cycles compound this problem, which they do for most girls. So parents may respond either by withdrawing or by verbally adding fuel to the fire just when their daughter most needs calm reassurance.

Definitely, no parent needs to tolerate a child's disrespect, and it's important to help her see how she's coming across. But in confronting these attitude problems, we want to stay in control, stay connected, and stay calm enough to work it through. We might say, "Honey, what you said was hurtful and unacceptable. Right now, we both need a break. When you are ready, I'd like you to try to explain more calmly why you are upset."

 In confronting these attitude problems, we want to stay in control, stay connected, and stay calm enough to work it through.

By making an effort to show love to a daughter who knows perfectly well that she's being disrespectful, we demonstrate that our support and love do not waver with her behavior—and in the process we provide reassurance that she is not rejectable.

A special note for moms.

Mom, when you see your daughter's dad hanging in there and loving her even in her most difficult moments, *thank him*! Since men, especially, are wired to go into warrior mode when they feel attacked, recognize that he's doing something that's *waaaaaay* outside his comfort zone. Tell him that you deeply respect his ability to hug the "porcupine" even in the face of perceived contempt.

You can also help your daughter see when her approach is infuriating Dad, perhaps pointing out how she would feel if her father behaved that way toward her. For example, "Kaitlyn, what do you feel when Dad is harsh and angry? Well, that's how he feels when you sneer at him. You're using words as weapons, and that is not what we do in this family. This is a chance for you to learn how to control what you say, so you don't develop habits that will hurt your husband and kids down the road."

The Engaging Woman Inside

Deep down, all girls know when they are copping an attitude with the parents who selflessly love them—and that guilty realization only adds to their secret fear that they aren't worthy of being loved. There's no quick fix. Yet day by day as you address the insecurities and behaviors that secretly plague your daughter, you can build her up to be the confident, strong, loving young woman that God created her to be—and that she deeply wants to be.

Eight

IN CASE YOU EVER WONDER...

What your child most wants to tell you

When I (Shaunti) found out that I was pregnant with my first child, a friend told me, "Having children means having your heart walk around outside your body for the rest of your life."

If you're like us, all the findings we've covered so far could leave you feeling a bit overwhelmed, especially since "having your heart walk around outside your body" can be so overwhelming anyway. When we look at our children, it's easy to slip into the universal parental worry about whether we're doing a good job, whether our kids will turn out okay, whether they have any concept of what we go through on their behalf, and whether they have any idea just how much we love them.

During seasons of difficulty, we may even wonder whether our children care about us at all.

But our research uncovered one more important finding: how our kids really feel about us.

The Number One Survey Response

We wanted to find out how all these highly opinionated, independent teens really think about their parents and the job they're doing. In our test surveys, we learned that asking that question directly invited flippant responses. So we upped the stakes. At the end of the real survey, we gave the kids a blank space and asked one open-ended question:

> Now we want you to imagine something very difficult.
> If you were to somehow find out that your parents were
> going to die tomorrow, what would you most want to
> tell them today?

Because the survey polled every conceivable type of teenager around the country, we still expected a significant number of frivolous comments or complaints. But as the hundreds of responses rolled in, it was impossible to read them without getting emotional. Because almost unanimously, the messages the kids sent read like this representative comment:

> Even though I have not acted like it all the time, I just
> want to let you know that I love you. Thank you for

pushing me to become the best person that I could possibly be. Even though I may have felt that you were being unfair, I realize now that it was all worth it, and that you did it because you love me.

Only a tiny fraction of the comments—less than 3 percent—were negative. Another small number of kids gave flippant answers or didn't respond at all. But the vast majority—95 percent—poured out an avalanche of heartfelt words, repeatedly saying, "I'm sorry," and, "I love you so much."

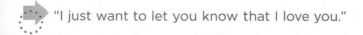 "I just want to let you know that I love you."

We could fill up another book with their wonderful responses (you can see many of them at www.forparentsonlybook.com), but here in alphabetical order are just a handful of comments that underscore what your child probably most wants you to know.

"I love and appreciate you, Mom and Dad."

- "Even after all we've been through, I still love you both. All I ever needed was to know that you were there for me. Thank you."
- "How much I love my mom and how much I appreciate her even when I act like I don't. She tries really hard, and I can act like a brat, but she means the world to me."

- "I am so sorry for everything I have done in the past. I realize I have made mistakes and have acted stupid lately, but I love you and respect your opinions."

- "I love you more than I let on, and even though we hardly ever agree I love you more than I can express. Thanks for trying to help even though I wouldn't let you."

- "I love you so much, and I'm sorry for all the times I've disappointed and burdened you in various ways. You were a great parent, even though I didn't tell you that more often. I can't wait to see you in heaven one day."

- "I would tell my parents that I love them so much, and I would cry all day telling them I'm sorry for every wrong thing I have ever done. I would tell them I wish this wasn't happening, and if I could, I would die for them. I would remind them many times that I love them more than anything, and they've helped me to live a happy life. I would let my parents know that they were successful in raising their child, and I would tell them I was happy that they are my parents."

- "I would tell them that I respect everything they have ever done for me and that without them I wouldn't be where I am today. I would tell them I love them, and I'm very sorry for all the hurtful things I have ever said to disrespect or disappoint them."

- "I would want to let them know that the opinions they have on things that affect me and my life are important to me, even if I don't like what they have to say. I would tell them that I love them, and that I would try to live my life the way they wanted me to all along. [And] even when I made my mistakes it was part of learning...and that they should rest assured that I would end up with a wonderful life because they cared."

- "I would want to tell them that I love them more than anyone else. I would want to thank them for allowing me to make my own life and for helping me to become the person I am and will be. I would want them to know that I will never forget them or what they have taught me. I would want them to know that I feel confident because of how they have raised me that I can get through anything and be okay. I want to thank them for the responsibility they give me and the trust they have in me."

- "I would want to tell them that I love them, and despite all the mistakes we both made, they mean the world to me, and I hope they feel the same."

- "I'm sorry for everything I have done. I feel like I've been a bad kid; please don't hate me. I love both of you very much. Please don't leave."

- "Mom and Dad, you'll never know how grateful I am that I am your son. Everything you've done for me, everything you've sacrificed, has not gone unnoticed. I love you both so much, and I wouldn't be the loving person I am without your love. Because of you both, I can survive in the real world. Despite all of our problems, you've guided me through them patiently, and now I'm stronger. I love you so much."

- "Mom and Dad, even though we've had issues in the past over stupid or even important things, and I've said things that probably hurt you and our bond, I love you more than everything, and I want you to know that. You have led me through every problem I have ever faced, including the ones you weren't even there for. Your life lessons and teachings over the years got me through those. Thanks for everything."

"Everything you've done for me, everything you've sacrificed, has not gone unnoticed."

- "Mom, I know that you worked very hard to raise me right so that I'd become a great man. I realize it's difficult raising four kids all by yourself and having a cruddy job, but I know you tried your best at everything you did, and I love you dearly for that. Thanks for being there when I needed you most."
- "Thank you for all the sacrifices you've made for me, I LOVE YOU, and thanks for always believing in me."

- "That I'm sorry for being mean. That I don't mean to be that way. I love them even if it doesn't show."
- "They are the best parents in the world. And because of them, I will become an outstanding citizen of the world. I will try to emulate them as much as possible in raising my children."

Be encouraged!

If you're like us, reading those survey responses is a six-hanky process. But we hope it is also encouraging. All of these comments came from the same kids whose survey answers confirmed their determination to fight for freedom and their own identity—and their tendency to cop an attitude with Mom and Dad from time to time. In other words…kids who probably look a lot like yours.

So even though it may not show right now, your child likely holds in his heart tremendous love, value, and respect for you. And one day he'll be able to tell you so. Like the biblical Proverbs 31 woman, you can cling to the expectation that your child will, eventually, "rise up and call [you] blessed."

The Best Is Yet to Come

We hope that what you have learned in these pages has given you fresh insight and inspiration for how you can not only connect with your exasperating, delightful child but also celebrate who he or she is becoming.

Most important, realize that even as you read these chapters and do the work that *you* can do, God is working too. Even more than you, he desires to see your children grow into amazing adults who fulfill his design and their callings to the fullest.

The teens we surveyed were pretty clear: if you'll hold on and persevere through these turbulent, wonderful, challenging, infuriating, and highly rewarding years, the results will follow. And someday, you may hear something like this final quote from a teenage survey-taker who shared what he would most want to tell his parents:

> I would tell them that I love them more than I've ever
> said or shown. That I appreciate their high standards
> for me, and their punishing me when I did something
> wrong. I would thank them for teaching me good values,
> theology, common sense, and manners. I would apologize
> for all the times I've held grudges against them or thought
> that they were being stupid or gave them trouble. I would
> make sure they knew that they are the most important
> people in my life, and they have made me who I am.
> That they've been my friends and counselors, and I appre-
> ciate all they've done for me. I would tell them that I'd
> miss them, and thank them for sharing their Christian
> faith with me so we have the assurance of meeting again.

Afterword

> Happy the generation where the great listen to the small, for it follows that in such a generation the small will listen to the great. —Hebrew proverb

Thank you for joining us on this journey inside the minds and hearts of kids. This book started out as an analytical project, but in the process of researching and writing, it became very personal to us as parents. We saw the truth of this Hebrew proverb come alive before our eyes, as we learned just how much our children *want* to share their lives with us—and to receive guidance from clued-in parents.

Kids really do want to talk. If you give them some pizza and Dr Pepper, kids will talk—for as long as you can listen. They'll answer just about any question you might have about how they feel, and they'll pontificate for hours, revealing themselves to be endless bastions of opinions...though you may not always agree with them.

As this project draws to a close, we've come to believe that we as adults miss so much richness with our kids just because we don't often take time to formulate good questions and really interview them. Or because we're scared to hear what they have to say.

We have to admit, that description fit us at times! But we found that when we approached kids with a mind-set like that of Jesus—unconditionally loving and nonjudgmental, yet also filled with Truth—we could handle almost anything they threw at us *and* have a better understanding of how to respond.

Despite all our surveys, statistics, and findings, we know that our own process of learning how to be good parents will continue for a lifetime. We're both making lists of the changes we want to pursue in our parenting, but in the end, we're extremely grateful that God's grace is what brings it all together to produce the amazing, fruitful adults our children will become. In other words, his ability to make it happen far outstrips our ability to mess it up! Is that good news or what?

Blessings as you—like us—continue this wonderful, scary, intense, and joyous journey.

—*Shaunti and Lisa*

Notes

Most of our research was primary research—going directly to the kids themselves in personal interviews or the national survey. The complete survey, including the verbatim answers to the final open-ended question, can be found at www.forparentsonlybook.com. And for readers who want to investigate specific parenting issues more deeply, we also list additional resources at that site, as well as at my (Shaunti's) central site: www.shaunti.com. Here are a few other citations:

Chapter 1

Cheaper by the Dozen, DVD, directed by Shawn Levy (2003; Los Angeles: 20th Century Fox, 2004).

Chapter 2

Sources for material on adolescent brain development:

N. Eshel and others, "Neural substrates of choice selection in adults and adolescents: development of the ventrolateral prefrontal and anterior cingulate cortices," *Neuropsychologia* (2007), www.nimh.nih.gov/press/adolescent-brains-risky-choices.cfm.

J. N. Giedd and others, "Brain development during childhood and adolescence: a longitudinal MRI study," *Nature Neuroscience* 2, no. 10 (1999), www.nature.com/neuro/journal/v2/n10/pdf/ nn1099_861.pdf.

Carolyn Y. Johnson, "Parents get look at teens' brains: Project seeks to explain behavior," *Boston Globe,* 10 November 2005, www.boston.com/news/education/higher/articles/2005/11/10/ parents_get_look_at_teens_brains?mode=PF. The advice of parents serving as the "external frontal lobe" comes from one of the scientists quoted in this article.

Chapter 3

References to stages of child development drew on Erik Erikson's Eight Stages of Development and other resources, including the following three: *Patient Teaching Loose-Leaf Library* (Springhouse, PA: Springhouse, 1990), http://honolulu .hawaii.edu/intranet/committees/FacDevCom/guidebk/ teachtip/erikson.htm and www.childdevelopmentinfo.com/ development/erickson.shtml. References to the "relativism" stage were clarified in interviews with Dr. Carbery.

Never Been Kissed, DVD, directed by Raja Gosnell (1999; Los Angeles: 20th Century Fox, 2003).

Deuteronomy 4:29: "But from there you will seek the LORD your
God and you will find him, if you search after him with all
your heart and with all your soul."

"Identity Circle," adapted from Mike Bickle's description,
www.ihop.org. Used by permission.

Chapter 4

"Put your big girl panties on and deal with it." This line can be
found in many places in popular culture and is also the title
of a book by Roz Van Meter (Naperville, IL: Sourcebooks,
2007).

Chapter 7

Quotes from Emerson Eggerichs regarding boys and respect are
drawn from a personal interview in August 2006 and from
quotes previously published in Shaunti Feldhahn, *For Women
Only* (Sisters, OR: Multnomah, 2004), 26.

Acknowledgments

As we look back at all the people who helped make this book possible, we are grateful for good friends, prayer warriors, parenting experts, and the real experts—the kids who lent us their wisdom in focus groups, interviews, and our scientific survey.

First, we'd like to express our heartfelt thanks to the members of the prayer teams that have prayed for us during this process: Martha and Barry Abrams, Diana Baker, Scott and Tammy Beck, Allan Beeber, Elizabeth Beinhocker, Scott and Patti Benjamin, Julie Blount, Mary Frances Bowley, Michael Brown, Ann and Tom Browne, Kathy Carnahan, Susan Conley, Christa Crawford, Gerry and Kasey Crete, Linda Crews, Johnny and Anne Crist, Alison Darrell, Mike Deagle, Debbie DeGraff, Zanese Duncan, Calvin and Nerida Edwards, Lynn and Craig Elam, Darby Ferguson, Julie and Scott Fidler, Susan Fleck, Sara Fogle, Larissa Fontenot, Nancy and David French, Meredith Gantt, Kate and Shad Gates, Dan Glaze, Deb and Michael Goldstone, Laura Grindley, Corkie Haan, Vance Hanifen, Dean and Jan Harbry, Leslie Hettenbach, Judy Hitson, Anne Hotchkiss, Parker Hudson, Lee Hultquist, Victor Jih, Jane Joiner, Lisa Joyce, Judy Keappler, Kelly Monroe Kuhlberg, Michael Leahy, Elsa Liebenberg, Mary Loudermilk, Jan and John MacLaury, Eve Montavon, Kurt Montavon, John and Lisa Nagle, Elizabeth Noller,

Bruce and Sue Osterink, Carla and Mike Owen, Betty and David Patten, Linda and Jack Preston, Molly Rankine, Dick and Judy Reidinger, Melba Rice, Annabelle and Mark Robertson, Roger Scarlett, Wendy and Albert Shashoua, D. J. Snell, Jacqueline Sweet, JoAnn Turbie, Jewels Warren, and Jennifer and Gene Wheeler.

And, for the fourth time, Chuck Cowan of Analytic Focus (www .analyticfocus.com) helped us design a stellar national survey, which was then conducted by the skillful team of Decision Analyst (www .decisionanalyst.com), especially Kelly Puig and Kevin Sharp.

We promised to keep the full names of the interviewees and focus group participants confidential, but we would like to thank, by first name only, several of the Atlanta-based focus-group kids, who went above and beyond in giving us not only great insights in their groups, but who allowed us to go back to them with questions, questions, and more questions as we got deeper into the research. Thank you so much Alexis, Amy, Andrew, Ben, Brandon, Chris H., Chris R., Christian, Christopher, Frank, Greg, Hannah R., Hannah S., Jered, Jessica, Jonathan, Joseph, Kimberly, Larry, Matt, Nate, Ryan, Sarah, Taylor, Tyler, Yotam, and Zachary.

A special thanks goes to Marsha Anderson-Bomar, who graciously allowed us the use of her offices at Street Smarts in Duluth, Georgia, to host many important focus groups, and to Marianne and Ron Murray, whose Atlanta Bread Company at The Forum in Norcross, Georgia, continues to act as a restaurant, an office, and an all-day conference room rolled into one.

Several experts were invaluable in providing assistance and help as we investigated the topics covered in this book. We'd like to especially thank Dr. Julie Carbery, Vicki Courtney (www.virtuousreality .com), Nerida Edwards, and Emerson Eggerichs (www.loveand respect.com).

We also could not have written this book without the personal and professional assistance we have received from Shaunti's hard-working staff team, including Vance Hanifen, Leslie Hettenbach, Keri Schuerman, Tally Whitehead, and most especially Shaunti's "right-hand man," Linda Crews—who was not only the first one to come up with the idea for this book, but by a twist of fate ended up as the cover model! We also must thank Zanese Duncan for her dedicated work in approaching potential endorsers, and, as always, we're so appreciative of the comprehensive insight and help of our agent, Calvin Edwards.

We owe extreme gratitude to the tireless and talented efforts of our editors, Laura Barker and David Kopp, and we also appreciate Steve Cobb, Dudley Delffs, and the whole WaterBrook Multnomah family for their spirit of excellence and grace—especially with high-maintenance authors like us. As we transition into the Random House world, we want to extend our fondest thanks to those of the "old" Multnomah family who have gone on to other things, especially Don and Brenda Jacobson. We miss you all, but you will always be very special to us.

We are so deeply grateful to our parents, Richard and Judy

Reidinger and Glen and Lee Hultquist, who beautifully modeled so many of the principles we're highlighting in this book. Thank you for your influence and continued encouragement in our work.

And there's no way we can adequately express our thanks to Jeff Feldhahn and Eric Rice, the most wonderful, supportive, encouraging husbands in the world. And we thank our six (combined) children for putting up with our crazy hours and schedules as we completed this book.

Most important, we want to humbly thank our heavenly Father, for we know that without him, the only perfect parent, we could have done none of this.